Evangelical Review of Theology

A Global Forum

Volume 45 • Number 2 • May 2021

Published by

Department of Theological Concerns

WIPF and STOCK *Publishers*
199 West 8th Avenue • Eugene OR 97401
wipfandstock.com

Great news—all issues of ERT dating back to 1977
are now available free on our website:
https://theology.worldea.org/evangelical-review-of-theology/
To order hard copies, contact orders@wipfandstock.com

ISSN: 0144-8153
ISBN: 978-1-6667-1784-6
Volume 45 • No. 2 • May 2021
Copyright © 2021 World Evangelical Alliance
Department of Theological Concerns

The free pdf of this journal is distributed under the following conditions:
The pdf may not be sold or used for profit except with written consent.
The pdf may be printed only for private use, not for profit.
The only printed copies that may be used in public are those obtained
from the publisher, Wipf & Stock.

General Editor: Thomas Schirrmacher
Executive Editor: Bruce Barron
Assistant Editor: Thomas K. Johnson
Book Review Editor: Peirong Lin

Committee
Executive Committee of the WEA Theological Commission
Dr Rosalee V. Ewell, Brazil, Executive Director
Dr Thomas Schirrmacher, Germany, Executive Chair
Dr James O. Nkansah, Kenya, Vice-Chair

Editorial Policy
The articles in the *Evangelical Review of Theology (ERT)* reflect
the opinions of the authors and reviewers and do not necessarily
represent those of the Editors or the Publisher.

The Editors welcome both unsolicited submissions and
recommendations of original or previously published articles
or book reviews for inclusion in ERT. Manuscripts, reviews,
queries and other communications may be addressed
to the Executive Editor at bruce.barron0@gmail.com.

Printed by Wipf and Stock Publishers
199 West 8th Avenue, Eugene, OR 97401
wipfandstock.com

Table of Contents

Introduction: Why We Need Theological Education 100

Sharing the DNA of Christianity 101
Thomas Schirrmacher, WEA Secretary General

Re-Forma: Solving a Key Issue in Global Training
of Pastors and Church Leaders 103
Manfred Waldemar Kohl

Cognitive Contextualization in Theological Education:
A Theoretical Framework 113
Richard E. Seed

Moving from Critical to Constructive Thinking 128
Perry Shaw

Can We Not Mourn with Those Who Mourn? 141
Walter Riggans

Holistic Mission in Biblical and Theological Perspective 152
Hannes Wiher

Reconciling God's Justice and His Sovereignty in the Process of Salvation:
Towards a Mediating View Between Causative Faith and Reprobation 164
Daniel Kirkpatrick

Luther's Peculiar Doctrine of the *Imago Dei* 176
Geoffrey Butler

Book Reviews 186

Introduction: Why We Need Theological Education

When I was writing about the 'health and wealth gospel' in the 1980s, other people said that any gospel that couldn't work in Africa was not the true gospel. I said they were wrong. Specifically, I said a 'prosperity' message could easily be transplanted to Africa, as long as the promises offered as part of the 'hundredfold return' were less grandiose than those dangled in front of itching ears in the United States.

Now, unbalanced forms of prosperity teaching have impacted Africa too. As a friend told me a few years ago, when I asked about its impact on that continent, 'Just go to Nairobi or Lagos and look at the billboards.'

One key reason for the spread of questionable teachings in Christian circles is the great number of pastors and leaders with limited theological training. We can't send every aspiring pastor off to school for three years, nor should we. But wherever we have influence, we can raise the expectations that those entrusted with Christian leadership will demonstrate theological maturity (see James 3:1).

This issue of *ERT* features articles from three people who have been influential in improving theological education, especially in the Global South. Manfred Kohl, founder of the WEA-affiliated effort to upgrade the quality of untrained Christian leaders, explains the rationale for his approach. Richard Seed digs deeply into the complex topic of teaching in a way that connects with the learners' context and provides real-life examples from Africa. Perry Shaw, who worked in the Middle East for 30 years, suggests important correctives to our love for 'critical thinking'.

This issue also contains a thought-provoking article on an imbalance in modern hymnody, plus theological articles that touch on three relevant topics: what the Bible says about holistic mission, God's justice in the process of salvation, and whether fallen humans retain the image and likeness of God. And we welcome a true lover of theology, Thomas Schirrmacher, as the World Evangelical Alliance's new Secretary General. Happy reading!

—Bruce Barron, Executive Editor

Letter to the editor

Wesley Hill's February article on the need for Christian unity, especially in the light of deep divisions over moral and ethical issues, was timely and important.

As he discussed the hot-potato issue of gay marriage, I found my biases surfacing and wanting to unpack what I see as weaknesses with 'the other side'. But to do that would go against the main point of the article: the need to find a way forward, to find that as-yet undiscovered country of 'common ground' where we can live in peace and reflect together from a different theological angle.

Hill fairly summarized his own view and the other side. My natural reaction was a desire to show what I consider the profound lack of serious exegesis on the opposite side from me. But I restrained myself and will continue to do so.

—Jim Reiher, Melbourne, Australia

Sharing the DNA of Christianity

Thomas Schirrmacher, WEA Secretary General

This article is excerpted and lightly edited from the message Thomas Schirrmacher delivered on his inauguration as Secretary General of the World Evangelical Alliance on 27 February 2021.

When Anglican priests and the Salvation Army started to work together in the nineteenth century, people thought that would not be possible. When German Lutheran pastors and professors invited Methodists from the United States to preach the gospel in Germany, that was unheard of.

Today, we are even more diverse confessionally, ethnically, and in language and culture. We have churches in the Brazilian rainforest where they worship ten meters above the ground in high trees, and we have churches on the 20th floor of skyscrapers in Malaysia.

What, then, does it mean to be evangelical?

Well, I can tell you one thing: evangelicals never agreed on politics! You can see this around the globe. There are countries with evangelical members in Parliament on the government side and in the opposition. We did not agree on politics in 1846 either. This is not the secret of the evangelical movement.

For me, to be evangelical implies enthusiasm for the DNA of Christianity. But this requires us to search for the DNA of Christianity.

For example, if someone questions whether the resurrection of Jesus or the story of Pentecost happened, we evangelicals stand for the historicity of our faith. But we do not treat this belief as something specific to us alone. Rather, we think it's the DNA of Christianity that we owe everything to what Jesus did and what the Holy Spirit does.

We are deeply convinced that the Bible is the confession of the Church. But the idea of a paper document that would rule the people comes from the Old Testament. For the ancient Hebrews, the Torah was above the king and everyone else. Some people mock us and say the Bible is our 'paper Pope'. We are proud to have a paper Pope, because it assures us that none of us, including me, are above the Word of God.

The Westminster Confession of 1647 states, 'The supreme judge by whom all controversies of religion are to be determined and all decrees of councils or opinions of ancient writers and doctrines of man and private opinions are to be examined and in whose sentence we are to rest, can be no other…'—and now you would expect it to say 'than the Scriptures'. But no! In 1647, they said the supreme judge 'can be no other but the Holy Spirit speaking in Scripture'. We believe the Holy Spirit is ruling His Church, but this is not *in opposition* to Holy Scripture. Rather, the Spirit is the author of the Holy Scriptures and is using His constitution, the Scriptures, to rule the Church. That for us is the DNA of Christianity and it is what evangelicals are all about.

Evangelicals have always emphasized that each believer should share the message that Jesus died on the cross for us and that only in Him can we find communion with God and eternal life. But let us look at the 2011 document 'Christian Witness in a Multi-Religious World', co-authored by the World Evangelical Alliance, the World Council of Churches and the Vatican. It begins by stating that 'mission is the very being of the Church' and speaks about every believer being obliged to witness to others about the gospel. Is this emphasis, then, specifically evangelical or is it generally Christian? It is Christian insofar as all churches agree now that mission is the very being of the church. This is the task that Jesus Christ handed to us. Insofar that not everybody is happy about putting it into action, it might be seen as a particular concern of evangelicals. But we have to be very careful about thinking that as evangelicals, we automatically do what Jesus said. Mission is not always the essence of our local churches. We evangelicals often have to be reminded as well to put witnessing to the gospel at the centre of our work.

As another example, let us consider religious freedom and persecution. In 1846, the World Evangelical Alliance was the first large religious body ever to speak up for religious freedom. That meant speaking up against state churches, against Christian nationalism—which is still a hot potato today even within our own ranks—and against the state pressing its religion and its thoughts on the people.

At the Second Vatican Council, the Catholic Church said exactly the same thing: that religious freedom is not just a political principle but part of the DNA of Christianity. So is this view evangelical? Well, we have stood for it for a long time. But we did not stand for it as a confessional item, but because we viewed religious freedom as an essential part of pure Christianity. God wants us to trust Him with our lives, but He does not want us to pray to Him because we are forced to or because someone paid us to do it. He wants our trust, our heart and our love, and love is something that cannot be forced.

So I am convinced that the evangelical movement stands up for specific things in the Christian world, but that these things are not specific in the sense that they are owned by us and distinguish us from others; rather, they are the DNA of the Christian faith itself. And when we strive for unity within evangelicalism, if we want to bring the Anglicans, the Pentecostals, the Reformed, the Salvation Army and all those groups in our midst together, we can do it only around the DNA of Christianity. We are open to any other church outside our movement joining us in affirming these aspects of Christianity's DNA, and we hope wherever possible to extend our vision to many other churches around the world.

Re-Forma: Solving a Key Issue in Global Training of Pastors and Church Leaders

Manfred Waldemar Kohl

An estimated two million evangelical pastors and church leaders worldwide lack formal theological training. Even if seminaries and Bible institutes had the capacity to educate them, few would have the time or resources to engage in full-time study. This article presents the solution offered by Re-Forma, an initiative affiliated with the World Evangelical Alliance.

A recent television advertisement showed a repair man standing in front of a poorly functioning dishwasher. The owner asked, 'What is wrong with my dishwasher? It's not working properly anymore. Is it the power, or the electronics, or how the dishes are being placed? Maybe some should be higher than others?' At the end of the ad, the repair man stated, 'You have to focus on the key issue—the right detergent. Without fixing this issue, nothing else will help.'

What is wrong with our churches and Christian ministries? We try new programmes, improve our entertainment emphasis, introduce great ideas about worship, and approve more committees, staff and funds. But still we are losing impact. The church has lost its prophetic voice as salt and light in society and is becoming increasingly insignificant and irrelevant. We know the problem is not the power; to blame the grace and power of our Heavenly Father would be completely wrong. So what is the solution? What are the key issues?

In March 2018, a group of evangelical church leaders and researchers met in Rome for one week to discuss the problem of nominalism in Christianity.[1] Today, millions of professing Christians are Christians in name only. Most of them were once active in the Christian community and in various ministries. They served on committees and participated in projects. Then they disappeared, and now one sees them in church only on Christmas or Easter if at all.

Since the conference was taking place in Rome, the organizers invited a representative from the Vatican to bring greetings. The person who came was

---

Dr. Manfred Waldemar Kohl is president of Re-Forma and ambassador for Overseas Council International, an organization that assists theological institutions primarily in the non-Western world. He also serves as catalyst for the Lausanne Network for Integrity and Anti-Corruption.

1 This was the Lausanne Global Consultation on Nominal Christianity, 14–18 March 2018. A summary of the consultation and its final statements can be found at https://worldea.org/yourls/ert452kohl1. A media release on the event is at https://worldea.org/yourls/ert452kohl2.

responsible for training priests, pastors, teachers, missionaries and Christian workers for the Roman Catholic Church. He indicated that in the Catholic Church, the greatest problem is that hundreds of millions of Catholics are Christians in name only. 'Lost sheep', he called them. To address this problem, he stated firmly, the training of pastors has to be changed. Training for ministry on all levels, he said, is insufficient in the area of outreach and relevant discipleship.

This message rang true with those gathered for the conference. It became very clear to all the conference participants that the key issue in solving the problem of nominalism in the church is proper pastoral leadership training. It seems that many pastors, teachers, missionaries and Christian workers have lost their understanding of being a shepherd as described by Jesus in John 10:1–18.

Having served on or frequently observed church committees appointed to find the right pastor for their church, I have noted that such committees seldom ask questions like 'What was the topic of your dissertation or main papers? Who were your advisors? What training and experiences do you have on caring for lost sheep?' Seldom do members of the search committee seek information on the candidate's previous performance with regard to shepherding believers and focusing on the lost. Moreover, the importance of inquiring into the candidate's prior demonstration of integrity in all spheres of life is rarely taken seriously. Usually, in a pastor search, the emphasis is on good preaching, strong administration and general creative oversight. This is especially true in large churches that have created the term 'lead pastor' for their top staff member.

Moreover, very few churches are actively involved in the various training institutes for pastors, missionaries and teachers. Ideally, they would not only support theological training centres with their prayers and financially but would also participate in discussions of the key issues those institutions are facing.

Over the last several decades, much has been written about the church and its needs in relation to the theological training programmes offered by seminaries and Bible institutes. Some foundations have invested time and funds in research,[2] recognizing that as the seminaries go, so goes the church.

The training of pastors, teachers, missionaries and Christian workers can be described in two categories: formal and informal (or non-formal) theological education. I will discuss each one below.

Formal theological education

There are approximately 900 registered evangelical seminaries in the world, accredited by eight regional or continental accreditation agencies. These agencies have established clear criteria for faculty and students with regard to curriculum, library and study tools, field work and practical involvement of students in the church. Most of these formal theological institutes are recognized by national

---

2   In 1994, the Murdock Charitable Trust interviewed 800 individuals who were in full-time ministry or attending church services regularly, asking them, 'What are the ten key issues that should be taught in theological training institutions?' The Lilly Foundation, the Pew Foundation and others have conducted similar research studies during the last decade.

governments as religious training institutions. Many hold a special status and qualify for tax exemptions.

How to improve formal theological education has been debated for centuries. Hundreds of books and dissertations have been written on the topic, and countless conferences, seminars and institutes have been held. This is the modern version of the ancient debate, 'What does Athens have to do with Jerusalem?'[3] or 'What emphasis should be placed on academic learning as opposed to the specific needs of the church?' Documents and manifestos have been written and adopted. Still, many churches led by pastors who were trained in formal theological institutions are losing their impact and relevance.[4]

Over the past decades, it has become quite clear that our formal theological training institutions must begin to change their curriculum, teaching methods and involvement with the church. The primary question, 'What are the relevant issues the church—and especially our youth—are facing today?' must be taken seriously. However, the term *change* usually embodies one of our greatest problems. One theologian wrote very critically about the problem of change in theological schools:

1. Theologians within theological institutions like to talk and debate, often with few results. It seems that action or change is to be avoided at any cost.
2. Theologians within theological institutions like to focus on the past; to plan ahead, deal with the needs of the church or think futuristically seems to be outside their comfort zone.
3. Theologians within theological institutions have difficulties with issues of practical ministry, management, fundraising and outcome-oriented assessment.[5]

Overseas Council International has convened several conferences in an effort to improve the relationship between the church and theological schools. In one of these conferences, 50 theology professors from different institutions, 50 pastors serving large and small churches, and 50 individuals who faithfully attended church every Sunday came together to discuss the health of the church. After two days a lady about sixty years old stood up, saying that she had never spoken to such a large group of people or used a microphone. Very nervously, she explained that she and her family were all followers of Jesus and involved in praying and regularly studying the Bible. She said she had belonged to her church since she was a child. She was baptized and married there and the entire family attended church every Sunday. She mentioned that over the last several decades the church had had four different pastors; pointing to one of the leading theologians in the group, she commented that all four had come from his institution. The conference went silent when she continued, 'All four

---

3 This ancient question was initially formulated by the North African church father Tertullian (c. 160–c. 220).
4 In Germany, for instance, the dissatisfaction amongst church people is alarming. In 2019 alone, 540,000 church members (both Protestant and Catholic) renounced their membership and are no longer paying the church membership tax, which is mandatory for members. See news reports in *IdeaSpektrum* 27 (2020): 6–7; *IdeaSpektrum* 29 (2020): 16–19.
5 Manfred Waldemar Kohl and A. N. Lal Senanayake (eds.), *Educating for Tomorrow: Theological Leadership for the Asian Context* (Bangalore, India: SAIACS Press, 2007), 41–42.

pastors were useless. Not one of them came to visit us or pray with us, even when we had a tragic death in the family. They never instructed us church members on how to reach out to others or be concerned about the lost. The terms "evangelism" and "outreach" were seldom mentioned. Their preaching went over our heads. It was mostly too difficult to understand.'

The woman then enumerated a long list of things she felt the pastors and their staff should have done. A healthy discussion followed and several of the other regular church attenders offered similar examples. At the end of the session, the head of that particular seminary was very shocked and embarrassed. He publicly apologized to the lady and asked her to give the same speech to his entire faculty and all the students preparing for ministry. He even invited her to become a member of the seminary's board.

We have to listen to these serious critical voices and recommendations. Unfortunately, very few people in our church have the courage to speak out. Happily, the situation is not all bad. Thousands of wonderful pastors are demonstrating a shepherd's heart in their preaching and are demonstrating biblically based mission outreach. Many churches today are growing and having an incredible impact in their town, city and country. These pastors have learned to go back to Scripture, as the subjects taught by Jesus and the method he used during his three-year 'seminary' for his disciples are still the most effective.

The International Council for Evangelical Theological Education (ICETE) is dedicated to helping the eight regional accrediting agencies and, through them, the over 900 evangelical seminaries around the world. It provides new initiatives to improve theological education. At the next global consultation of ICETE (scheduled for November 2021), a specially appointed committee plans to present a proposed new manifesto (with clear points of implementation) for formal theological education. We hope that it will be ready for general discussion at the following ICETE global consultation in November 2022. This is an important moment, because effective theological education is needed more than ever to train leaders for today's and tomorrow's church. Whatever needs to change must be changed, since without change there can be no improvement.

This is not the first such undertaking. In 2000, Overseas Council International (OCI), under the leadership of John Bennett, Steven Hardy and myself, formed the Institute of Excellence. For the last 22 years, OCI has held institutes annually in each of 10 regions of the world, bringing leaders of theological schools together for one week to deal with issues they are facing and to learn from experts how to develop relevant solutions. For many of them, the Institute of Excellence was a very effective pathway to bring changes into formal evangelical theological education.

We have dealt with some key questions: What are the issues that today's church is facing, and how can we train the next generation of pastors to deal with them? What new courses must be added to the curriculum and what should be dropped? How can we move from theory to practical, relevant ministries? We have also dealt with very complex questions such as how to respond to the constant requests to create more PhD programmes, elevate theological seminaries to university status, and combine biblical studies with other areas of learning. We grappled honestly with whether such changes actually helped the church or were more related to matters of personal pride and institutional status. As Marvin Oxenham, in his excellent book on character and virtue,[6] has stated, in theological education the emphasis should be not only on knowing and doing but also on *being* what Scripture says, with a focus on sound knowledge, skills and character.

Informal or non-formal theological education

Todd Johnson, director of the Center for the Study of Global Christianity, has stated that only 5 percent of all pastors or priests in Christian churches worldwide have a formal theological education and an officially recognized theological degree. More than 90 percent have received only some kind of informal education; some have received no training at all. About two million evangelical pastors, teachers, missionaries and Christian workers belong in this larger group.

Globally, there are at least 40,000 (and possibly closer to 100,000) informal theological training programmes. There are Bible colleges, mission schools, leadership training programmes, Internet-based courses and international pastoral training institutes in virtually every country. A study in the Philippines listed more than 370 official established training programs in that country alone; actually, there are hundreds more.[7] Every mission agency or Christian organization in the world has its own training programme, and so do most megachurches. The number of informal or non-formal programmes increases daily.

In some cases, seminaries with formal theological programmes have been asked to help with informal programmes.[8] Several excellent informal programmes exist under the umbrella of 'Pastors Training Pastors', an initiative started by RREACH (led by Ramesh Richard of Dallas, Texas; www.rreach.org). This organization held a 'Global Proclamation Congress for Pastor Trainers' in 2016 near Bangkok, Thailand, with excellent follow-up activities. RREACH works in conjunction with the Trainers of Pastors International Coalition (TOPIC; www.topicglobal.org), where Al Bridges serves as global facilitator.

GACX (www.gacx.io), a global alliance for church multiplication with 99 churches and mission agencies as members, predicts a global growth of several million new churches within the next decade. Clearly, established seminaries could never fill the anticipated need for leaders of these churches. Rather, thousands of additional informal theological training initiatives must be created.

Whereas formal theological education has a clearly defined programme, curriculum, exams, degrees and associated accreditation processes, the thousands of informal programmes have nothing similar: no guidelines, no standards, no outcomes that could be globally accepted and recognized. Each one does what it

---

6   Marvin Oxenham, *Character and Virtue in Theological Education: An Academic Epistolary Novel* (Carlisle, Cumbria, UK: Langham Global Library, 2019).
7   Manfred Waldemar Kohl, *The Church in the Philippines: A Research Project with Special Emphasis on Theological Education* (Manila, Philippines: OMF Literature Press, 2005), 22–31.
8   As an example, BEST, a seminary in Bangui, Central African Republic, regularly invites leaders and teachers of Bible schools and other ministry training programmes in the country to attend a week of lectures as well as offering mentorship and other forms of assistance. The entire BEST faculty is involved in this activity on a regular basis, with encouragement and financial support from Overseas Council International and other organizations.

considers best. Quite often, the concepts and beliefs of the founders or leaders of each denomination or mission agency determine how the various training programmes are carried out. One teacher and missionary leader stated publicly that he had personally trained more than 15,000 pastors for ministry; each pastor received about six weeks of training and then the missionary leader ordained them as pastors. He and his board believe that such training is sufficient. There are countless such examples around the world. We would all be better off if all the informal training programmes for evangelical church leaders had clear, globally recognized guidelines or standards, focused on biblically based outcomes.

The ministry of Re-Forma

As vice president for Overseas Council International, with the responsibility of assisting theological institutions in the non-Western world, I had the privilege of visiting and working with nearly 500 institutions, both formal and informal. Some are very good; others are not. But when I was confronted with the fact that over 90 percent of all pastors, teachers, missionaries and Christian workers have not been trained in a formal theological institution, I felt an incredible burden. I discovered that the single biggest dilemma in Christianity today is the problem of poorly trained or completely untrained pastors and leaders.

We cannot solve this problem by multiplying the capacity of formal theological education tenfold. That would not be feasible; in most of the world, Christian leaders lack the time or resources to devote two or three years to study. Rather, establishing specific, meaningful guidelines or international standards for people in ministry—an essential baseline for everyone involved in Christian leadership—seemed to be the best answer. It does not matter whether someone has attended a mission school or Bible institute for three years, done coursework online, or completed an intensive programme of self-study. What matters is the outcome—whether the person has achieved baseline standards of preparedness for biblical ministry. Such internationally recognized, outcome-based standards, which can be applied to Christian leaders without formal theological training, have never existed.

To fill this gap, in 2016 I founded Re-Forma (www.re-forma.global). I started by calling together a group of experts from around the world on the training of pastors and church leaders. Our main purpose was to establish a succinct, easily understood set of ministry standards that could be applied to Christian leaders globally. Re-Forma became legally registered in Germany in 2019, and then in South Africa in 2020; we plan to achieve registration in North America, Asia and Latin America over the next three years. Reuben van Rensburg serves as Re-Forma's full-time project director, with additional staff at several locations.

Re-Forma exists for the following reasons:

1. To establish guidelines and globally recognized, outcome-based standards for all biblical ministries.
2. To help and encourage existing global and local training programmes that are not part of formal training institutions by providing a list of needed subjects of instruction and outcomes.

3. To provide any person or institution fulfilling the required outcomes with a certificate of biblical training for ministry, which is underwritten by the World Evangelical Alliance.
4. To provide the same Re-Forma biblical ministry guidelines and outcomes that could be used for new believers, new churches and especially any new training programs.
5. To enhance the effectiveness and reach of the many existing training institutions and programmes, as well as the quality of networking amongst them.

For Re-Forma, the key issue is that every pastor or church leader should have a solid, biblically derived knowledge base that is applicable to every main aspect of Christian ministry.

Re-Forma has established 35 basic outcomes that every person in Christian ministry should master. These 35 outcomes are simple and readily measurable. A Bible college, mission school or Internet-based programme can apply these outcomes as part of their curriculum or teaching material. Even individuals can achieve these outcomes on their own. The Re-Forma outcomes can easily be transferred to an orality-based culture and its people.

The best analogy to the Re-Forma approach is to consider what happens when someone wants to obtain an official driver license. Applicants are not asked what training school they attended, who taught them, or how much time they spent learning to drive. Rather, they are given a test (typically including both written and actual driving components). The underlying question is 'Show me that you can drive properly and that you know all the important traffic requirements.' Re-Forma is taking the same approach. It is asking 35 key questions to determine whether a person knows how to do biblically based Christian ministry.

Every candidate who applies for a Re-Forma certificate is tested by a qualified local facilitator who has attended a Quality Assurance Institute. Re-Forma brings the facilitators together in various countries or regions to train them in administering the Re-Forma outcome examination to groups of graduates. Quite often, the leader or principal of a training programme also serves as facilitator. These trainers are already familiar with the Re-Forma guidelines and, in many cases, are building their instructional programmes around those guidelines.

Some of Re-Forma's 35 outcomes are listed below:

1. **Knowing the Scriptures**
    1.1 Recount 10 of the main events in the Old Testament and share the stories of at least 10 of the main characters in the Old Testament.
    1.2 Explain by using five examples how Jesus fulfils Old Testament prophecy.
    1.3 Summarize at least five major teachings of Jesus.
    1.4 Explain why the death and resurrection of Jesus are so important.
    1.5 Explain the significance of Jesus' relationship with his disciples for discipling others today.

1.6 Describe 10 main events in the book of Acts.
1.7 Explain at least three of Paul's key teachings.

2. Living by Faith
2.1 Describe the fruit of the Spirit in all areas of your life, including how to practise integrity, simplicity and humility.
2.2 Which are the two spiritual disciplines you struggle with most and what are you doing about it?
2.3 List three ethical values and principles that are of vital importance to the well-being and future of a congregation and explain why.
2.4 Explain how you demonstrate compassion, welcome and forgiveness in all your relationships, including relationships with people who have special needs.
2.5 How do you practise kindness and hospitality?

3. Outreach
3.1 What would you see as the one or two most important obstacles in your church and your culture, with regard to sharing the gospel in private and public?
3.2 Describe how you mentor at least one person in a specific form of evangelism or mission.
3.3 Explain why the Bible is more important than culture. List three examples where your culture and surrounding society would greatly benefit if, instead of following their cultural practices, they would listen to and follow biblical values and standards.
3.4 Describe how you have identified and trained at least three others to serve in some form of church leadership.
3.5 How do you demonstrate servant leadership? Indicate how you would explain, to someone in your church who thinks that a church leader should be honoured and that others should serve him or her, why Jesus acted differently and why this is important from a Christian view of church hierarchy.

4. Listening and Encouraging
4.1 How do you comfort and assist others in times of crisis, personal problems, illness or death?
4.2 How do you help a couple prepare for their marriage, marital problems, family issues and illness?
4.3 Recount at least seven stories in the Bible where God used children.
4.4 Explain how Jesus' attitude towards children should change the church.
4.5 Describe the impact of absentee fathers and what must be done to produce change and healing.

5. **Trustworthy Faith**
    5.1 Why is sound doctrine important?
    5.2 Which in your opinion are the major doctrines a new Christian should understand as soon as possible and why?
    5.3 Explain three of the most important events in the history of the Church.
    5.4 Highlight five New Testament passages that urge believers to give generously to ministry.
    5.5 Explain why the prosperity gospel is unbiblical and unethical.
    5.6 List five examples that highlight the importance of the Church.

Re-Forma provides additional material and commentary related to each of the 35 questions/outcomes. It also offers materials and guidelines for pastors and church leaders who have a newly established training programme or plan to establish one.

Just as formal theological education needs to deal with the key issue of finding and communicating biblically based answers to the relevant issues the church is facing today, the key issue for informal programmes is to establish a unified standard for biblical ministry. Re-Forma offers such a standard—a baseline founded on biblical principles. These outcomes-based standards could also be useful to formal theological institutions, and to the countless pastors who finished their formal theological training years ago but have never had time for further study (except reading commentaries for their sermons). The 35 Re-Forma outcomes could make a helpful ministry refresher course or form a continuing education for any pastor.

Re-Forma plans to identify local representatives in most areas of the world. Its material has already been translated into 20 languages. The leadership of Re-Forma (board, staff and advisory council) comprises more than 40 theologians and church leaders from around the world.[9]

Conclusion: resolving another key issue

The reports of new believers and new churches being formed in some parts of the world today are astonishing. They reflect God's grace and his blessing of faithful mission and outreach efforts. But they also suggest that we need to develop more than a million additional pastors and church leaders every year![10]

About five decades ago, Billy Graham had a burden for evangelism and outreach. For several years, he gathered key theologians and church leaders with the goal of developing a new global approach to evangelism. Participants included the British theologian John Stott; Anglican Bishop A. J. Dain from Sydney, Australia; the American theologian and editor of *Christianity Today*, Carl Henry; Donald Hoke, founding president of Tokyo Christian College; American evangelist Leighton Ford and others. During these meetings, each person presented their understandings of global evangelism and outreach, and long discussions ensued.

---

9   All staff, board and advisory council members are identified on the Re-Forma website, www.re-forma.global.
10 See GACX, 'Going Further Together' (video), https://worldea.org/yourls/ert452kohl3 and information from the GProCommission, www.rreach.org.

After much debate, it was agreed to call a World Congress on Evangelism for all evangelical leaders. More than 2,600 came to the Swiss city of Lausanne in 1974.[11] The impact and blessing were enormous. All participants went home with a renewed commitment to bring the gospel to everybody, everywhere. Evangelism became the language as well as the direction of evangelical Christianity. The Lausanne Covenant, with Stott as its chief architect, has been regarded by many as the most significant missions document produced in the modern Protestant era.[12] Today we can rejoice in what has been accomplished, but there is still much to do.

The need to greatly increase the number of biblically trained pastors and leaders must be taken more seriously by all mission agencies, church planning organizations, training institutes and parachurch agencies. As South African theologian and missionary leader Stephanes Sigemindus Loots stated, at a meeting that Ramesh Richard and I convened in March 2021 to discuss how to address this need, 'Church planting is moving at the speed of a bullet train, with leadership development following on a bicycle.' A global leadership summit should be called for the purpose of finding, training, mentoring and commissioning a million women and men for the needed ministries every year. It is hoped that from the outset these additional training efforts could be based on the outcomes and global standards established by Re-Forma.

To close, let us hear once more from the dishwasher repair man, reminding us to focus on the key issues. For formal theological education, a key issue is to be more relevant to the church's needs. For informal or non-formal theological education, a key issue is to have a baseline of globally recognized standards, which Re-Forma has now established. For all evangelical churches and organizations, a key issue is to train millions of additional pastors and leaders for biblical ministry, pursuant to the mandate Christ gave us in Matthew 9:36–38: 'The harvest is plentiful but the workers are few.'

---

11 The best summary of the origin of the Lausanne conference and the subsequent Lausanne movement is J. E. M. Cameron (ed.), *The Lausanne Legacy: Landmarks in Global Mission* (Peabody, MA: Hendrickson, 2016), especially the foreword by Leighton Ford. See also J. D. Douglas (ed.), *Let the Earth Hear His Voice. A Comprehensive Reference Volume on World Evangelization* (Minneapolis, MN: World Wide Publications, 1975); Manfred Waldemar Kohl, 'The Beginning of the Lausanne Movement', *Haddington House Journal* (forthcoming 2021).
12 Julia E. M. Cameron, *The Lausanne Covenant: Complete Text with Study Guide* (Peabody, MA: Hendrickson, 2011).

Cognitive Contextualization in Theological Education: A Theoretical Framework

Richard E. Seed

One inescapable reality of our connected and globalized world is the diversity and plurality of the human situation into which the Word of God speaks. This diversity arises from the living matrix within which each individual is nurtured and is evidenced in the learning and cognitive structures used to build understanding. This article investigates ways to deal with these realities and create cognitively contextualized theological education.

When asked to comment on their theological training, a group of pastors in Africa made a deeply concerning observation. They agreed that in their theological training, neither the African mind nor the urban informal or rural contexts in which they were now ministering had been properly addressed. They were well taught in Hebrew and Greek, exegetical method and the traditional disciplines of theology, but once in the parish they struggled to see how these impacted the lives of their church members. It had taken them some time after graduation to connect with their congregations and build a ministry and mission strategy for their contexts.

Sadly, from these pastors' perspectives, the African mind had simply not been addressed in their training. The problem was that the curriculum to which they had been subjected as students lacked *cognitive contextualization*. In this article, I explore a theoretical framework that will assist theological educators to fill this gap.

In the 1980s, Harvie M. Conn began to discuss the relationship between theology, anthropology and mission. He proposed that the three had initially been held in close proximity to each other but had later diverged under the influence of relativism.[1] For Conn, the way forward in addressing issues of contextualization was to reclaim the agenda of anthropological research in a 'missionary anthropology'.[2] He called for a new paradigm, illustrated by the works of Charles Taber, Alan Tippett, Jacob Loewen, Eugene Nida, Paul Hiebert and Charles Kraft, in which an

---

Richard E. Seed (PhD, University of Birmingham) is director of Theological Education Development Services, which provides training, support and consultation to seminaries and Christian universities in Africa. He also lectures at George Whitefield College in South Africa, has authored journal articles on learning in theological education, and was a contributor to and co-editor of *Is Africa Incurably Religious? Secularization and Discipleship in Africa* (Regnum, 2020).

1 Harvie Conn, *Eternal Word and Changing Worlds: Theology, Anthropology and Mission in Trialogue* (Phillipsburg, NJ: P&R Publishing, 1984), 76.
2 Conn, *Eternal Word and Changing Worlds*, 138.

interdisciplinary, three-way dialogue is created between the social sciences, theology and missiology.³

In addressing what this interdisciplinary dialogue should mean for theological education, Conn endorsed Gerhard Kittel's position that 'each Bible teacher must seek to apply to the life of the individual and to the life of the church in the world the truth of God's Revelation.' Conn added the caveat that this cannot be accomplished in isolation from the cultural world the theological educator is addressing.⁴ Although Conn did not adequately show how this dialogue between theological education and anthropology can be achieved, he pointed us in the right direction with his concept of trialogue between theology, social science and mission.

The tools theological educators need to carry this trialogue forward and achieve effective cognitive contextualization lie in the cross-disciplinary nature of their work. The field of mission studies calls theological education to address issues raised by contextualization and the relationship between mission and theology. From anthropology, theological education draws insights into the human context; from research into higher educational practice, it builds its particular understanding of learning and teaching. The theoretical principles of cognitive contextualization are therefore drawn from the three distinct but overlapping disciplines of missiology, cultural psychology and anthropology, and education.

Cognitive contextualization as a missional issue for theological education

The theological foundation for cognitive contextualization lies in the recognition of the centrality of mission for theology and therefore also for theological education. More specifically, it lies in the missional dynamics of contextualization.

One of the major movements in theological thinking of the twentieth century is the assertion that mission is definitive for theology. Several missiologists argue that since theology is essentially missionary, theological education should reflect this. David Bosch did much to relink theology with mission.⁵ He was followed in this path by Andrew Kirk, Robert Banks, Bernard Ott, Chris Wright, Steve De Gruchy and Robert McCoy.⁶ The point of unity between mission and theological education is in

---

3   Conn, *Eternal Word and Changing Worlds*, 183.
4   Conn, *Eternal Word and Changing Worlds*, 301–2.
5   David J. Bosch, 'Theological Education in Missionary Perspective', *Missiology* 10, no. 1 (1982): 13–34; Bosch, *Transforming Mission* (Maryknoll, NY: Orbis, 1998).
6   Andrew J. Kirk, *The Mission of Theology and Theology as Mission* (Valley Forge, PA: Trinity Press, 1997); Kirk, *What Is Mission? Theological Explorations* (London: Darton, Longman and Todd, 1999), 75–95; Robert Banks, *Re-envisioning Theological Education: Exploring Missional Alternatives to Current Models* (Grand Rapids: Eerdmans, 1999); Bernard Ott, *Beyond Fragmentation: Integrating Mission and Theological Education* (Oxford: Regnum, 2001); Steve De Gruchy, 'Theological Education and Missional Practice; a Vital Dialogue', in *Handbook of Theological Education in World Christianity: Theological Perspective—Regional Surveys—Ecumenical Trends*, ed. D. Werner, D. Esterline, N. Kang and J. Raja (Eugene, OR: Wipf and Stock, 2010), 43–51; Michael McCoy, 'Restoring Mission to the Heart of Theological Education', in *Handbook of Theological Education in Africa*, ed. Isabel Apawo Phiri and Dietrich Werner (Oxford: Regnum International, 2013), 523–30; Chris Wright, 'Rooted and Engaged', *Evangelical Review of Theology* 38, no. 4 (2014): 324–38.

the sending of the Trinity, which results in a mission-centred understanding of what it means to be the church. The church is missionary by its very nature because it is a product of the prior mission of the Trinity.[7] The agenda for all theology and its goals are therefore set by the church's concern for the mission of God, or *missio dei*. The Lausanne movement echoes this emphasis when it states, 'The mission of the Church on earth is to serve the mission of God and the mission of theological education is to strengthen and accompany the mission of the church.'[8] Part and parcel of this relationship between theology and mission is the relationship between cultural contexts and the gospel. In contemporary thinking on mission, this relationship is considered under the rubric of contextualization.[9]

The current concern for contextualization as an aspect of mission has its historic antecedents in both Roman Catholic and Protestant mission practice. In the past, Roman Catholic mission thought sought to relate the gospel to various cultures by changing liturgies, vestments, some rites, art, architecture and music to reflect local customs. These efforts were designated by such terms as adaptation and accommodation. Protestants, on the other hand, tended to address this issue using the concept of indigenization. This approach is best illustrated by Henry Venn and Rufus Anderson,[10] who anticipated local churches being governed, propagated and supported by the local community.

In 1972, Shoki Coe and the Theological Education Fund (TEF), a division of the World Council of Churches, used the term 'contextualization' to broaden the scope of the gospel to include the socio-political aspect of life.[11] In so doing, they sought to move thinking on the relationship between the gospel and context beyond the earlier contributions of missiologists such as Venn.[12] Coe and the TEF envisioned widening the scope of the engagement between the gospel and human contexts to account for God's involvement in human history so as to bring about racial, social and economic liberation. However, others from evangelical and Catholic persuasions diverge from Coe and from each other in their conceptualization of the term. David Hesselgrave points out that these endeavours have grown out of existing theological bents and matrices that have in large measure determined their results: 'The different theological orientations—orthodoxy, liberalism, neo-orthodoxy, and neoliberalism—tend to yield very different definitions of contextualization.'[13]

In the face of these multiple conceptualizations, Catholic scholar Stephen Bevans provides a 'catch-all' definition of contextualization 'as a theology that takes human

---

7   Bosch, *Transforming Mission*, 372.
8   Lausanne Movement, *A Confession of Faith and a Call to Action* (2011), https://worldea.org/yourls/ert452seed1.
9   Stephen Bevans and Roger Schroeder, *Constants in Context: A Theology of Mission for Today* (Maryknoll, NY: Orbis, 2004), 386; Bosch, *Transforming Mission*, 433–67; Kirk, *What Is Mission?* 118–43.
10 Wilbert Shenk, 'Henry Venn and Mission Thought', *Anvil* 2, no. 1 (1985): 25–42.
11 Shoki Coe. 'Contextualizing Theology', in *Mission Trends 3*, ed. Gerald H. Anderson and Thomas Stransky (Grand Rapids: Eerdmans, 1976), 21
12 Brian De Vrees, 'Towards a Global Theology: Theological Method and Contextualization', *Verbum et Ecclesia* 37, no. 1 (2016), http://dx.doi.org/10.4102/ve.v37i1.1536.
13 David J. Hesselgrave and Edward Rommen, *Contextualisation: Meanings, Methods and Modes* (Leicester, UK: Apollos, 1989), 144.

experience, social action, culture, and cultural change seriously'.[14] Contextualization is a theology, an articulation of perceptions of God that are not isolated from human existence but embedded in it. Bevans categorizes the different approaches to this task under six models. In the 'translation model', contextualization is the faithful conveying of the unchanging gospel message in terms that are understood in ever-changing and particular contexts. The 'anthropological model' emphasizes the preservation of cultural identity by a person of faith. The term 'praxis model' denotes approaches to contextualization that focus on social change. Those who try to provide a balance between the models already mentioned are classified as using the 'synthetic model'. The 'transcendental model' is grounded in Western philosophy, in which the starting point is one's own religious experience and experience of oneself. Finally, the 'countercultural model' looks at the context with suspicion, raising questions and calling for appropriate U-turns of mind and practice.

One early evangelical adopter of contextualization was Byang Kato,[15] who is said to have introduced a modified understanding of the concept to the evangelical community through the Lausanne Congress on World Evangelization in 1974.[16] Evangelical conceptualizations of contextualization give biblical tradition and confessional statements a controlling role. The gospel and the written texts need to be conveyed and understood as clearly as possible in different cultures and languages.[17] Evangelicals, therefore, usually reflect a strong leaning towards a translation model of contextualization.

Two major evangelical contributors to this discussion from the late 1970s were Charles Kraft and Bruce Nicholls. The latter reflected many of the same concerns as Kato. Kraft, meanwhile, did not engage directly in discourse on contextualization but was nevertheless influential in this area. Kraft's concern was to convey Christian meaning across cultures and languages by moving away from word-to-word equivalence to a more dynamic approach that involves the equivalence of meaning. To convey this idea, he adopted the terms 'Dynamic Equivalence' and later 'Meaning Equivalence' in Bible translation and worship practice.[18] In so doing, he pointed us in the direction of linguistics, culture and cognition as concerns to address when translating the Christian message.

Today, many evangelicals go beyond this emphasis on linguistics and translation and adopt a more synthetic approach. For these scholars, contextualization is a process of dynamic dialogue in which universal, transcendental and eternal gospel

---

14   Steven Bevans, *Models of Contextual Theology* (Maryknoll, NY: Orbis, 2008), 27.
15   Keith Ferdinando, 'The Legacy of Byang Kato', *Africa Journal of Evangelical Theology* 26, no. 2 (2007): 3–12.
16   Paul Bowers, 'Theological Education in Africa: Why Does It Matter?' *Africa Journal of Evangelical Theology* 26, no. 2 (2007): 134–50.
17   Bruce J. Nicholls, *Contextualization: A Theology of Gospel and Culture* (Vancouver, Canada: Regent College Publishing, 1979).
18   Kraft's relevant works include *Christianity in Culture* (Maryknoll, NY: Orbis, 1979), 64–77; 'Supracultural Meanings via Cultural Forms', in *A Guide to Contemporary Hermeneutics*, ed. Donald K. McKim (Grand Rapids: Eerdmans, 1996); *Communication Theory for Christian Witness* (Nashville, TN: Abingdon Books, 1991); *Anthropology for Christian Witness* (Maryknoll, NY: Orbis, 1996), 135–37; *Appropriate Christianity* (Pasadena, CA: William Carey Library, 2005), 155–69.

values are embedded in local, imminent and temporal human societies.[19] They would further agree with a summary of contextualization as 'an ongoing process where the gospel is assimilated into the total life of a people in their cultural context so that the message makes sense to those who profess it'.[20] They would, however, add a clause recognizing individual and social transformation as the goal of contextualization.[21] This understanding contains a counterentural element or, as Paul Hiebert terms it, 'critical contextualization' as culture and historic context are both affirmed and challenged by the gospel.[22]

Contextualization is more than linguistic translation and implies the transference of the message of Christ into life through the result of transformed cultural practice and values which are returned to God as worship. It has a strong discipleship element and is directed at allowing believers to follow Christ while functioning within their own culture.[23] Contextualization is therefore a process rather than a product. At the heart of the process are understanding and knowledge that inform and transform life. Furthermore, through this process a knowledge of God is constructed. When this process is raised to a conscious level, it takes on the form of self-theologizing. Bevans is therefore right to define contextualization as theology. It is an understanding of the divine–human relation fashioned not simply on the artifacts of the human context and culture but from within its deepest structures of thought. However, an element of cultural relativism is also at work in this process. Cultures and societies are not uniform with regard to how they construct their world. To achieve the goal of effective contextualization, theological education needs to recognize the role of culture and context in shaping the thought structures through which self-theologizing is formulated.

Cognitive contextualization as an issue for cultural cognition

Contextualization is about being in culture. Language, social practices, values and worldview are all cultural creations and are therefore pertinent to the contextualizing task of a missionary theology. The second set of theoretical foundations for cognitive contextualization lies in insights from the social sciences, particularly when they describe aspects of the relationship between the group, culture and cognition.

Behind much sociological research lies the assumption that psychological development takes place as a person participates in social interactions and culturally

---

19 Scott A. Moreau, *Contextualizing the Faith: A Holistic Approach* (Grand Rapids: Baker, 2018), 3; Timothy Tennent, *Theology in the Context of World Christianity* (Grand Rapids: Zondervan, 2007), 11–13.
20 J. B. Bangura, 'The Gospel in Context: Hiebert's Critical Contextualisation and Charismatic Movements in Sierra Leone', *Die Skriflig* 50, no. 1 (2016).
21 Orlando E. Costas, *Liberating News: A Theology of Contextual Evangelization* (Grand Rapids: Eerdmans, 1989), 31.
22 Hiebert addressed this issue in *Anthropological Reflections on Missiological Issues* (Grand Rapids: Baker, 1994); 'Critical Contextualization', *Missiology: An International Review* 12 (1984): 287–96; 'Critical Contextualization', *International Bulletin of Missionary Research* 11 (1987): 104–12.
23 Jackson Wu, *One Gospel for All Nations: A Practical Approach to Biblical Contextualization* (Pasadena, CA: William Carey Library, 2015), 277.

organized activities. Cognition is seen as part of psychological development and therefore as influenced by the society in which one is nurtured. Human societies are not all the same, so cultural variations can result in cognitive variations.[24] The idea that human psychological development is achieved through being enmeshed in a socio-cultural world has significance for the relationship between culture and cognition.

There is a reciprocal relationship between culture and cognition

Viewing the correlation between culture and cognition brings their dynamic relationship into focus. Sperber and Hirschfeld see the relationship as reciprocal: culture is about cognition, but cognition is also about culture. Culture, for the most part, is created by and gives expression to human cognitive abilities.[25] Culture in turn is made possible by cognitive capacities.

Culture has a pedagogic function

In this culture–cognition dynamic, culture functions pedagogically. The teaching method is through participation in 'culturally mediated, historically developing, practical activity involving cultural practices and tools'.[26] By simply growing and developing within a society, doing what the society does and using what it uses, individuals are nurtured through a semi-conscious enculturation and socialization process into the ways, habits and thinking of a society.

Culture provides the individual with cognitive frameworks

Through this teaching process, individuals learn the structures they use to think about, understand and function in the world as a member of the group.[27] An individual's knowledge structures are therefore shaped by culture-sensitive cognitive frameworks.[28] These frameworks all have durations in time and space that extend beyond the individual and exist in a culture's collective cognition. This 'cultural cognition' is the source of most of an individual's knowledge, perspectives, attitudes and opinions. Furthermore, these socially generated interpretive schemes are used in day-to-day life and function for the individual as ready-made heuristics.

Cognitive contextualization recognizes the close relationship between culture and cognition and that cognition is not simply what happens 'between the ears' but also involves society, culture, context and interaction between persons. Four culturally mediated frameworks are significant for cognitively contextualized

---

24 Dan Sperber and Lawrence Hirschfeld, 'Culture, Cognition, and Evolution', in *MIT Encyclopedia of the Cognitive Sciences*, ed. Robert Wilson and Frank Keil (Cambridge: MIT Press, 1999), cxi–cxxxii.
25 Sperber and Hirschfeld, 'Culture, Cognition and Evolution', cxv.
26 John Gatewood, 'Cultural Models, Consensus Analysis, and the Social Organization of Knowledge', *Topics in Cognitive Science* 4 (2012): 362–71.
27 Serge Moscovici, 'The Phenomenon of Social Representations', in *Social Representations*, ed. Robert Farr and Serge Moscovici (Cambridge: Cambridge University Press, 1984), 3–68; Moscovici, 'Why a Theory of Social Representations?' in *Representations of the Social: Bridging Theoretical Traditions*, ed. Kay Deaux and Gina Philogene (Oxford: Blackwell Editors, 2001), 8–35.
28 Michael Cole, *Cultural Psychology: A Once and Future Discipline* (Cambridge, MA: Harvard University Press, 1996).

theological education: (1) language, which provides tools for cognitive development;[29] (2) a community's conceptual framework;[30] (3) perceptual modes and cognitive pathways;[31] and (4) a values or worldview framework by which a community constructs the complex and flexible ways in which it thinks and feels.[32] We will review these four separately.

The four culturally mediated frameworks

Language

There is little doubt that language is an artefact of culture. However, what is the relationship between language and cognition? This discussion extends back into the mid-twentieth century with the observations of Whorf and of Brown and Lenneberg.[33] From Whorf comes the Sapir-Wolf hypothesis, which suggests that the particular language spoken by a person determines how that person thinks about reality. Most scholars would tone down 'determines' to 'influences' in that hypothesis, but as cognitive linguist Ronald Langacker reminds us, language is 'an essential aspect of the conceptual apparatus through which we apprehend and engage the world'.[34]

Neuroscience suggests that we have distinct but interrelated cognitive and language hierarchies. The cognitive hierarchy cannot be learnt without language, whereas the language hierarchy is 'acquired from the surrounding ready-made language the learning of which is grounded in communication with other people'; throughout life, 'language guides acquisition of cognitive representations from experience.'[35] It is therefore required for the development of cognition and 'has a profound effect on thought', causing some distinctions between the thinking of different groups and providing schematic modes for thought.[36]

The relationship between language and cognition raises important questions for theological educators, such as these:

- What is the role of mother-tongue theological teaching for theologizing?
- What support and sensitivity are required by people learning in a second or third language?

---

29 P. Wolf and K. Holmes, 'Linguistic Relativity', *WIREs Cognitive Science* 2, no. 3 (2011): 253–65.
30 Farzad Sharifian, *Cultural Linguistics: Cultural Conceptualizations and Language* (Amsterdam and Philadelphia: John Benjamins, 2017).
31 Richard Nisbett, *The Geography of Thought* (London: Nicholas Brealey, 2011).
32 Bert Peeters, Kerry Mullan and Christine Beal, 'Introduction', in *Cross-Culturally Speaking: Speaking Cross-Culturally*, ed. Bert Peeters, Kerry Mullan and Christine Beal (Newcastle-Upon-Tyne, UK: Cambridge Scholars, 2013), 1–10.
33 Benjamin Lee Whorf, 'An American Indian Model of the Universe', *International Journal of American Linguistics* 16, no. 2 (1950): 67–81; R. Brown and E. Lenneberg, 'A Study in Language and Cognition', *Journal of Abnormal and Social Psychology* 49, no. 3 (1954): 454–62.
34 Ronald Langacker, 'Culture, Cognition and Grammar', in *Language Contact and Language Conflict*, ed. Martin Pütz (Amsterdam: John Benjamins, 1994), 25–53; Ronald W. Langacker, *Cognitive Grammar: A Basic Introduction* (Oxford: Oxford University Press, 2008).
35 Leonid Perlovsky, 'Language and Cognition', *Neural Networks* 22 (2009): 247–57.
36 Wolf and Holmes, 'Linguistic Relativity'.

- How do those teaching biblical languages relate to the students' mother tongue without going through a European language?
- What efforts are made to create mother-tongue learning resources?

There is no one answer to these questions, since the needs of theological students and the characteristics of theological institutions vary so greatly. However, the questions must not be ignored.

A community's conceptual framework

Cultural conceptualization[37] is the communally accepted interpretation of, approaches to, reactions to or understanding of experiences and stimuli that form part of the shared experience of a community. This is the way a culture sees the world through a common lens and expresses these commonalities in its use of language. When these experiences are commonly shared, the resulting perceptual lenses become dynamic systems of knowledge, which in turn act as major anchor points for people's thoughts and behaviours and can thus construct a worldview. Cultural conceptualizations are not static but 'are constantly negotiated and renegotiated across generations and are given life in cultural artefacts'.[38]

Cultural conceptualizations are bound up in the language that a community uses and emerge through interactions between members of a cultural group.[39] Farzad Sharifian describes the construction of cultural conceptualizations through a hierarchical taxonomy of increasing complexity. Cultural schemes are the pools of knowledge shared by the members of a speech community; cultural categories are the agreed-upon way in which items of knowledge are classified and contain a variety of schemes; cultural metaphors are overarching maps or models that allow members of a community to connect multiple aspects of life, linking them in a way that is consistent with their worldview. Cultural conceptualizations affect cross-cultural interactions, not only between language groups but even between social classes, political viewpoints or age cohorts within a single language group.

Cultural conceptualizations raise important issues for cognitive contextualization in theological education. The key is that the learning experience must be delivered at the level of the cultural conceptualization of the community being taught. To achieve this, curriculum design must have a high degree of insider input. It should therefore be undertaken as a collective and collaborative effort, and the teaching experience itself should allow for a high degree of autonomy, democracy and ownership. This allows the gospel to address cultural issues that a particular community may face—such as the influence of traditional perceptions of power in the role of a bishop, the role of the spiritual world in healing and prosperity, concepts of honesty or family, or where cultural conceptualizations create theological blind spots.

---

37 Farzad Sharifian, *Cultural Linguistics: Cultural Conceptualizations and Language* (Amsterdam and Philadelphia: John Benjamins, 2017), 10.
38 Sharifian, *Cultural Linguistics*, 17.
39 Sharifian, *Cultural Linguistics*, 252.

Perceptual modes and pathways

The third aspect of cultural cognition is the culturally and linguistically mediated structures for the cognitive processes of individuals. In the middle of the twentieth century, research in various disciplines indicated that the logic of various cultures was not identical.[40] This led David Hesselgrave to propose that people attain knowledge through three different modes: conceptual and formal logic, concrete relational connections, and physical experience.[41] Differences in cognitive processes are the result of differences in the way these modes are mixed in the thinking process. Subsequently, Richard Nisbett's comparative research on American and Chinese students has supported the notion of culturally mediated differences in logical structures. He observed that Chinese students perceived the world on the basis of interconnecting relationships from a big-picture perspective whereas North American students focused more on analysing the characteristics of the parts. From these observations, he distinguishes between two culturally mediated logic processes, i.e. holistic and analytic cognition.[42] This distinction has been corroborated in research into Japanese culture and cognition.[43] Nisbett explains this distinction on the premise that socio-economic and cultural factors affect cognitive habits. He contends that ecology, economy, social structure, attention, metaphysics and epistemology all influence cognitive processes.[44]

In seeking to be cognitively contextualized, theological education strives to understand the learning structures and patterns of its students. This requires focused research. In the African context, we have a few good examples, such as Earle and Dorothy Bowen's effort to incorporate students' learning styles in their theological instruction. My own research reviewed Nigerian theological students' approaches to texts.[45] Teaching practices should be constantly modified through reflective practice and honed both to resonate with the students' learning approach and to build learning capacity.

---

40 Edmund Perry, *The Gospel in Dispute* (New York: Doubleday, 1958), 99–106.
41 David Hesselgrave, *Communicating Christ Cross-Culturally: An Introduction to Missionary Communication* (Grand Rapids: Zondervan, 1991), 289–340; Hesselgrave and Rommen, *Contextualisation*, 205–6.
42 R. E. Nisbett, K. Peng, I. Choi and A. Norenzayan, 'Culture and Systems of Thought: Holistic versus Analytic Cognition', *Psychological Review* 108, no. 2 (2001): 291.
43 Richard E. Nisbett and Y. Miyamoto, 'The Influence of Culture: Holistic versus Analytic Perception', *Trends in Cognitive Sciences* 9, no. 10 (2005): 467–73.
44 Richard E. Nisbett, *The Geography of Thought: How Asians and Westerners Think Differently and Why* (London: Nicholas Brealey, 2011), 33–39.
45 Dorothy Bowen, *Cognitive Styles of African Theological Students and the Implications of These Styles for Bibliographic Instruction* (PhD thesis, Florida State University, 1984); Earle A. Bowen, *The Learning Styles of African College Students* (PhD thesis, Florida State University, 1984); Richard E. Seed, 'The Use of Text in Theological Education in Nigeria', *Discourse: Learning and Teaching in Philosophical and Religious Studies* 9, no. 2 (2010): 243–71.

Worldview and values frameworks

In the 1980s, Geert Hofstede began researching the cultural dimensions on which a society's values could be plotted and how these values relate to behaviour.[46] Hofstede proposed several dimensions along which cultural values may be analysed.[47] Subsequently, Shalom Schwartz developed three dimensions of culture while Trompenaar and Hampden-Turner saw cultural values as diverging along a seven-dimension construct.[48] This work was extended by the 'globe project', which significantly expanded Hofstede's cultural dimensions.[49] Although Hofstede and Trompenaar are concerned with corporate and national culture, the notion of cultural dimensions is used more generally and is found in research on leadership training, cross-cultural communication and education. In education, Hofstede's dimensions are used to create a 'Cultural Dimensions of Learning Framework' that lists the spectrum of cultural value differences impacting teaching and learning.[50]

From the above discussion, we can see that contextualizing theological education requires theological educators to recognize the importance of cultural cognition in its effect on language, conceptualization, cognitive structures, and worldview. Each of these factors impacts the cognitive process and causes variation in students' thought progressions. For the theological educator, applying the implications of cultural cognition means identifying issues of concern, exploring solutions through reflective practice, and adapting teaching practice accordingly. In the next section, we will see that theological educators can look to research on student learning in higher education contexts for help in locating these cultural issues in their actual practice of curriculum development and instruction.

Cognitive contextualization as an issue for educational psychology

Having explored the big picture of culture and learning, we will now narrow the focus to the level of the individual in constructing understanding. This is the level at which theological educators can influence student learning and allow our students

---

46 Geert Hofstede, Gert Jan Hofstede and Michael Minkov, *Cultures and Organizations: Software of the Mind*, 3rd ed. (New York: McGraw-Hill, 2010); Geert Hofstede, 'Dimensionalizing Cultures: The Hofstede Model in Context', *Online Readings in Psychology and Culture* 2, no. 1 (2011), http://dx.doi.org/10.9707/2307-0919.1014; Geert Hofstede, *Culture's Consequences: Comparing Values, Behaviors, Institutions, and Organizations across Nations*, 2nd ed. (Thousand Oaks, CA: Sage, 2001); Geert Hofstede, *Culture's Consequences: International Differences in Work-Related Values*, 2nd ed. (Beverly Hills, CA: Sage, 1984).
47 Hofstede, *Cultures and Organizations*.
48 S. H. Schwartz, 'Universals in the Content and Structure of Values: Theoretical Advances and Empirical Tests in 20 Countries', *Advances in Experimental Social Psychology* 25 (1992): 1–65, https://worldea.org/yourls/ert452seed2; Fons Trompenaar and Charles Hampden-Turner, *Riding the Waves of Culture: Understanding Cultural Diversity in Business* (London: Nicholas Brealey, 1998).
49 Kristin Piepenburg, *Critical Analysis of Hofstede's Model of Cultural Dimensions* (Munich: GRIN Verlag, 2011), https://worldea.org/yourls/ert452seed3.
50 Patrick Parrish and Jennifer A. Linder-VanBerschot, 'Cultural Dimensions of Learning: Addressing the Challenges of Multicultural Instruction' (2010), https://worldea.org/yourls/ert452seed4.

to extend their learning capacity beyond their natural ability. For this we can turn to insights from education research and in particular the work of Marton and Säljö.[51] From their research into university students' learning practices, they developed the notion that students approach their learning in one of two ways, which they call 'surface' and 'deep'. A third category, the 'achieving learning approach', has been added by John Biggs and Noel Entwistle.[52] The surface approach sees learning as banking facts; in contrast, the deep approach views learning as creating personal meaning, and the achieving approach sees the learning task as gaining maximum success by working strategically. Various researchers have developed these basic notions into a body of research with its own tools and methods, known as 'Student Approach to Learning' (SAL).

Proponents of this approach to educational research perceive learning as a process in which contextual and existential factors interact to produce a learning outcome. A student's cultural conception of learning is a contextual factor that orients a student's learning towards a surface- or deep-level outcome. In his presage–process–product model (3Ps), John Biggs provides an analytical structure for teaching and learning in which we can plot the influence of culture on learning.[53] Moreover, he gives us a tool to analyse the relationship between students' prior experiences, their approaches to learning and the quality of their learning outcomes.

Presage factors are the latent factors that, when activated in the learning process, direct the process of learning and its eventual outcome. They encompass two main subcategories: student factors and teaching and institutional factors. In both subcategories, societal and cultural influences play a significant role. In the *process* phase of this model, the presage factors are brought into a dynamic and fruitful relationship in the learning experience and steer the learning process using two points of reference. The first of these is students' perceptions of the learning context at hand, which are shaped by the interaction between the students' previous experiences of learning and the present context.[54] The second is their culturally mediated conception of what the task of learning requires. In this way, language, conceptualization, worldview and perceptual processing (the four frameworks we examined in the previous section) are all brought into the learning moment. Finally comes the *product* or outcomes phase, in which qualitative differences in outcomes are associated with qualitative differences in approaches to learning.[55]

A particular factor that has excited much interest is the role students' conceptualizations of learning play in their learning processes. Over the years, a number of culturally specific research projects have examined this issue in Australia,

---

51 F. Marton and R. Säljö, 'On Qualitative Differences in Learning: Outcomes and Processes', *British Journal of Educational Psychology* 46 (1976): 4–11.

52 John Biggs, 'Individual and Group Differences in Study Processes', *British Journal of Educational Psychology* 55 (1978): 185–212; Noel J. Entwistle, M. Hanley and D. J. Hounsell, 'Identifying Distinctive Approaches to Studying', *Higher Education* 8 (1979): 365–80.

53 Biggs, 'Individual and Group Differences in Study Processes'.

54 M. Prosser and K. Trigwell, *Understanding Learning and Teaching* (Buckingham, UK: Open University Press, 1999).

55 F. Marton and R. Säljö, 'Approaches to Learning', in *The Experience of Learning: Implications for Teaching and Studying in Higher Education*, ed. F. Marton, D. Hounsell and N. J. Entwistle, 2nd ed. (Edinburgh: Scottish Academic Press, 1997), 39–58.

Asia, Africa, Europe and the United States. This research has been particularly interested in the connection between students' conception of learning, their approach to learning and the outcome of that learning.[56] Behind this research is 'a basic proposition that "conceptions of learning" are not an isolated aspect of "prior knowledge", but that they are related to the interaction between cultural and experiential factors in a student's psychological development. These conceptions of learning influence what a student thinks is required in a given learning context.'[57] They are also relatively stable characteristics that, together with contextual factors, influence students' approach to learning.[58]

Furthermore, we know that people's conceptions of learning are not universal but relative. Säljö concludes, 'To learn is to act within man-made institutions and to adapt to the particular definitions of learning that are valid in the educational environment in which one finds oneself.'[59] Different educational environments define learning according to different socially and culturally established conventions with respect to what counts as learning. When there is a discrepancy in conceptualizations of learning between the teacher and student, the student experiences a dissonance that is detrimental to learning outcomes.

Biggs encourages us to apply these findings to the construction of learning in higher education using an outcomes-based approach.[60] In this method, the educator identifies where the learning is going and where students are currently, and then he or she works out what the learning experience must include to get students to the desired destination. Identifying learning outcomes is primary. Next, the context of the learner, which includes his or her culturally conceptualized perceptions and approaches to learning, is considered. Then, the content, methods, activities and questions are deliberately designed to engage the students at the level of their culturally mediated learning frames and encourage them towards a high level of cognitive involvement with the material.

For the theological educator, whether in a cross-cultural or intra-cultural context, the following concepts drawn from this approach are useful:

- Learning is seen as a process in which contextual and existential factors interact to produce a learning outcome.

---

56 B. Dart, 'Teaching for Improved Learning in Small Classes', in *Teaching and Learning in Higher Education*, ed. B. Dart and G. Boulton-Lewis (Melbourne: Australian Council for Educational Research, 1998), 222–49; F. Marton, 'Describing and Improving Learning', in *Learning Strategies and Learning Styles*, ed. R. Schmeck (New York: Springer, 1988), 53–82.
57 J. H. F. Meyer and G. M. Boulton-Lewis, 'Variation in Students' Conceptions of Learning: An Exploration of Cultural and Discipline Effects', *Research and Development in Higher Education* 20 (1997): 481–87.
58 John T. E. Richardson, 'Approaches to Studying, Conceptions of Learning and Learning Styles in Higher Education', *Learning and Individual Differences* 21, no. 3 (2011): 288–93.
59 Nola Purdie and John Hattie, 'Assessing Students' Conceptions of Learning', *Australian Journal of Educational & Developmental Psychology* 2 (2002): 17–32; R. Säljö, 'The Educational Construction of Learning', in *Student Learning*, ed. J. T. E. Richardson, M. W. Eysenck and D. W. Piper (Milton Keynes, UK: Open University Press, 1987), 106.
60 John Biggs and Catherine Tang, *Teaching for Quality Learning at University* (Maidenhead, UK: Open University Press, 2011).

- Student learning in the classroom is a bottom-up process in which a student's cultural cognitive frameworks and perception of learning play formative roles.
- This process is not solely determined by the natural gifting of the student but is susceptible to being influenced by factors found in the learning experience that the teacher provides.
- The process of curriculum and lesson construction moves from knowing the learning outcome, to knowing the presage factors that influence learning, and then to building the learning experience with these in mind to achieve the desired outcome.

In identifying the outcomes for theological education, we will diverge from the concepts of the SAL school, which emphasizes outcomes in terms of surface and deep learning. In theological education, in harmony with the missional nature of theological education, we define outcomes in terms of theological and biblical perspectives. However, we can appropriate from the SAL school the realization that culture directly impacts the learning process and the construction of individual understanding. Furthermore, we can note its emphasis on carefully constructing the learning experience in a way that is sensitive to cultural conceptualizations, but that takes the student past whatever limitations might be contained in those frameworks towards a learning process that delivers a high level of cognitive engagement as its outcome. In this work, the theological lecturer should draw from scholarship on teaching and learning, through an intentional process of inquiry, so as to improve his or her instructional and assessment practices and thereby improve student learning.

Cognitive contextualization in practice

In this section, I attempt to demonstrate the value of the preceding theoretical considerations by offering a few examples of teaching practice that reflect the recommended trialogue with mission, anthropology and education at a practical level.

Establishing a training programme for pastors using a collaborative curriculum process

A theological education consultant was asked by the leadership of an African Independent Church (AIC) to develop a training curriculum for pastors. To do this, the consultant followed the principles of collaborative curriculum development, in which lecturers develop the curriculum collectively. The process began with brainstorming sessions incorporating the church's leadership and theological educators who would teach the course. The aim of this phase was to identify exactly where the programme should go in order to address the context of the church's mission. The context was defined as comprising three components: the context of faith, the context of mission and the context of leadership. This led to the selection of the courses for the programme, which were directly linked to building student capacity to function in these contexts. Once the subject areas were identified for the curriculum, each subject was further described in terms of specific learning outcomes and content, which were again linked with the categories of faith, mission and leadership.

Reflecting some years later, the leaders who had commissioned the curriculum and provided funding for its implementation remarked on the visible impact the training had had on church growth. Graduates of the programme had planted a large number of church congregations. At the congregational level, local congregations expressed a preference for congregations to be led by the graduates of this programme, as they were the pastors most able to minister to the people's needs.

Combining the group dynamics of peer teaching and feedback in resource-based learning

A lecturer teaching Old Testament subjects at an institution in Rwanda adopted a group-based strategy for teaching. Groups of students were provided with self-study material that consisted of outlines, basic concepts, case studies and library research activities. The students worked through their assigned activities, which were relevant to their context, required identifying and solving problems that were raised and gave them opportunities for group and individual library research. Once they had worked through the materials in groups, the whole class came together again. In the classroom, basic concepts were rehearsed and the groups gave informal presentations. Issues of cognitive contextualization addressed in this experiment included group communal orientation to learning and engagement with the material at the level of cultural conceptualization. The course also strengthened students' academic skills and their ability to extract information. As a result, the students in this class petitioned the college administration to deliver all their lessons in this way, as they felt comfortable learning in groups and also appreciated the scaffolded approach taken to develop their library and academic skills.

Using problem-based learning structures to teach history

A lecturer teaching African church history at a Kenyan university approached teaching a course from the cultural conceptualization of time that valued both the present and past. Students were given an assignment to research their own family and clan history of engagement with Christianity. They were required to use living sources of oral accounts and to locate relevant artefacts such as letters and baptism certificates. These personal histories were presented orally in the class. The presentations raised a range of historical issues, such as relationships with missionaries, breakaway movements, circumcision debates, and issues related to specific tribes and oath taking, amongst others. Students engaged in further library research to examine these issues and fill in the broader historical context. Aspects of cognitive contextualization addressed in this experiment were concepts of time, community identity, a cognitive pathway that started with the concrete context, oral strengths, and use of the mother tongue. It also strengthened academic skills in the use of primary sources and evidence to construct historical accounts. End-of-course evaluations elicited comments such as 'This was no ordinary church history course. You made our history come alive.'

Conclusion

Theological education needs to consider three disciplines in its trialogue. The first and foremost is the theological essentials that belong to an evangelical understanding of mission and contextualization. These provide the framework and goals of the theological enterprise. The second consists of insights, tools and skills drawn from cultural anthropology and cross-cultural psychology that assist in identifying how the teaching function of the church can extend the love of God into multiple human contexts. The third is scholarship on teaching and learning, as we apply insights from research on education to build Christian teaching in such a manner that those trained express their Christian faith in a culturally appropriate way.

The need for cognitively contextualized theological education is not limited to non-Western contexts. It is relevant in all cultures, including Western culture, where secularism and post-modernity increasingly provide the dominant identity narratives, values and cognitive structures. No students should leave a theological education programme believing that their culturally mediated cognition has not been addressed in the course of study.

New WEA Theology Books Online

Peter Lawrence's *Fellow Travellers* is a fascinating comparative study of the identity development experienced by messianic Jews, Arab evangelicals and Muslim-background believers in the Holy Land. Lawrence shows that although the three groups have face unique challenges and follow very different paths in their spiritual development, they have a strong sense of connection and belonging when they encounter each other as fellow evangelical believers.

Thomas K. Johnson, senior advisor to the WEA Theological Commission, has released two books. *The Protester, the Dissident and the Christian* is a collection of nine essays on human rights issues. *Humanitarian Islam, Evangelical Christianity, and the Clash of Civilizations: A New Partnership for Peace and Religious Freedom* examines the tenets of the Indonesia-based Muslim movement with which the WEA is collaborating and explains the reasons for this partnership.

These books and all others in the WEA World of Theology Series and Global Issues Series can be downloaded at https://www.bucer.de/ressourcen/wea-cd.html.

Moving from Critical to Constructive Thinking

Perry Shaw

The author, based on his 30 years of experience in cross-cultural education and on biblical interpretation, warns that an over-emphasis on critical thinking can foster sub-Christian understandings of such concepts as autonomy and tolerance. He proposes an approach more typical of collectivist societies, in which students balance their development of a critical voice with respect for accumulated community wisdom.

In education, the words we use matter. The terms we choose can shape the ethos and mood that pervade the learning space. One widely used term in education in the Minority World[1] is *critical thinking*. Although I recognize the value of critical thinking, I will argue in this article that the language of 'constructive thinking'[2] provides a healthier trajectory, especially for the Majority World, than the language of critical thinking that has been inherited from academia in the Minority World.

My perspective is shaped by 30 years of cross-cultural immersion as a missionary educator, with a particular focus on Christian training in the Middle East, primarily the Arab Baptist Theological Seminary. Over the last 15 years, I have been a consultant and trainer in theological schools across the Majority World. During that time, I have been deeply concerned by the following observations:

- The legion of complaints from leaders of Majority World schools as to the arrogant dismissal by visiting Minority World lecturers of the quality of their school and their students.
- The expectation of visiting lecturers that students elsewhere in the world should follow Minority World patterns of knowledge construction, often without any awareness of the long and rich legacy of local knowledges.[3] In particular, the circuitous and indirect approaches of narrative reasoning

---

Perry Shaw is Researcher in Residence at Morling College, Sydney, and author of *Transforming Theological Education*. Prior to moving to Australia, Perry served in the Middle East for 30 years, including an extended period as professor of education at the Arab Baptist Theological Seminary in Beirut.

---

1 I prefer 'Minority World' rather than the more common 'West' or 'Global North' to emphasize that the Western perspectives often treated as normative actually represent assumptions developed by a minority culture as to the appropriate underpinnings of educational priorities.
2 By 'constructive thinking' I do not mean to allude to constructivist understandings of learning, but to an approach to thinking and action that seeks to build up the community through positive and productive outcomes.
3 César Lopes, 'Nurturing Emancipatory Local Knowledges', in *Challenging Tradition: Innovation in Advanced Theological Education*, ed. Perry Shaw and Havilah Dharamraj (Carlisle, UK: Langham, 2018), 145–65.

that are so foundational to thinking in much of the Majority World are often summarily dismissed.[4] Likewise, the strong heritage of spiritual engagement that undergirds much of African and Asian society is viewed by many Minority World teachers as a substandard framework for theological work, rather than as a pathway towards growth in discipleship.
- An assumption that Minority World approaches to critical thinking are the best way to achieve a healthy church life and accomplish God's mission. It is particularly ironic when instructors from contexts where the church is struggling to survive despise more vernacular approaches to teaching and learning used in contexts where the church is growing rapidly.

An upcoming collection focused on cross-cultural Christian training,[5] which includes 30 reflections from across the globe, has identified as its central theme the need for Minority World instructors teaching in the Majority World to engage in 'humble listening'. Even more striking is the advice offered by several of the papers to teachers coming from elsewhere: 'Don't come!' The strong feelings based on negative experiences of perceived arrogance from outsiders are palpable.

In the Middle East, many of our students come from highly collectivist societies in which respect for elders is paramount and expressing open criticism of existing leaders can cause young graduates to be distrusted or even ostracized. This is another reason why the indiscriminate importation of Minority World understandings of critical thinking can have profound negative consequences.

These experiences have forced me to reflect on the largely unquestioned value of 'autonomous critical thinking' that I experienced in my own studies, and on whether a more holistic outcome for Christian higher education might be found—one that would be more relevant and impactful in Majority World contexts. I realize that many Minority World teachers, especially those steeped in the European philosophical heritage, may have difficulty understanding the issues at stake for Majority World educators. Accordingly, my primary audience for this article is the leaders of theological colleges in the Majority World. My interest in reaching them motivated me to publish this essay in the World Evangelical Alliance's theological journal. Of course, if Minority World educational leaders could benefit from listening in on this conversation, I would be quite pleased.

As I noted above, this is not a broadside against critical thinking. I see much value in the training I have received, and in fact I will be using a form of critical thinking in this paper to critique critical thinking! I contend not that critical thinking is wrong *per se*, but rather that in our Christian educational endeavours we need to temper its use with humility in community and seek wisdom through richer and more constructive approaches to learning.

---

4 Stephanie Black, 'Scholarship in Our Own Words: Intercultural Rhetoric in Academic Writing and Reporting', in Shaw and Dharamraj, *Challenging Tradition*, 127–43.
5 Perry Shaw, César Lopes, Joanna Feliciano-Soberano and Bob Heaton (eds.), *Christian Training Across Cultures: A Global Perspective* (Carlisle, UK: Langham, in press).

Defining 'critical thinking' is problematic

Due to the ongoing hegemony of the Minority World academy, the revered learning outcome of critical thinking has been exported across the globe. Critical thinking is frequently prominent amongst our desired educational goals, even in theological education. The term is ubiquitous in Western education, even though many students seem to have only a vague understanding of what it means.

The concept of critical thinking is extremely murky. Brett Hunt describes it as 'paradoxical', asserting that you generally cannot understand critical thinking until you know how to do it.[6] In some of the better-known tests of this skill, such as the Cornell Critical Thinking Test or the Sample Reasoning Mindset Test, it seems to centre on the ability to resolve logical syllogisms. In most popular usage, however, critical thinking clearly encompasses some elements that we should seek to promote:

- The ability to engage in a balanced evaluation of sources.
- The ability to differentiate between factual, normative, interpretive and causal statements in the development of arguments.[7]
- The ability to discern logical and illogical thought patterns in what one reads or hears.
- The ability to place an issue in the broader context of ideas and practices.
- The ability (to borrow Bloom's taxonomy) to move from mere knowledge and understanding to more complex analytic, synthetic, evaluative and creative thinking.
- The ability to develop an argument that considers multiple perspectives and goes beyond surface-level quoting and dichotomistic statements.

Overall, critical thinking is generally viewed as a necessary individual skill and predominantly, if not exclusively, as a cognitive exercise.

Many students confuse critical thinking with just being critical, as if critical thinking requires finding fault in others. This problem is exacerbated when the term is translated literally into other languages, particularly when the local term used for 'critical' has strongly negative connotations. In some cases, a somewhat conflictual classroom environment results. Some Minority World teachers welcome what they see as robust debate in the classroom, but for those with greater relational sensitivity, notably those from more collectivist societies, such discussions are often perceived as aggressive, antagonistic, disunifying and hence unhelpful. I will return to this issue later.

Historical background

The contemporary Minority World emphasis on the development of critical thinking skills exists for good reason. Although recognition of the importance of critical thinking dates back to ancient times, events of the twentieth century—

---

6   Brett Hunt, 'Unpacking the Critical Thinking Conundrum', *The Teaching Professor* 32, no. 7 (2018): 1, 7.
7   Jennifer Fitzgerald and Vanessa Baird, 'Taking a Step Back: Teaching Critical Thinking by Distinguishing Appropriate Type of Evidence', *PS: Political Science and Politics* 44, no. 3 (2011): 619–24.

especially two catastrophic world wars, the Cold War and numerous other conflicts—have contributed to a profound suspicion of authority figures. Our promotion of critical assessment reflects a healthy desire to avoid the tragic consequences that have often followed mindless obedience to authority and conformity to questionable cultural norms. More recently, the echo chambers of social media and the rise of populist leaders have made it even more crucial for us to assess critically the material we hear and see.

In the realm of education, probably the most significant influence on contemporary understandings of critical thinking was John Dewey. He consistently stressed the importance of 'reflection', which he defined as the 'active, persistent and careful consideration of any belief or supposed form of knowledge in the light of the grounds that support it and the further conclusion to which it tends'.[8] Perhaps even more significant in recent years has been Paulo Freire, who embraced the importance of developing a 'critical pedagogy' as a pathway to empower the oppressed and disenfranchised.[9] Abusive relationships exist where personal individuality is denied, and critical evaluation can be a crucial factor on the road to liberation and justice.

In short, there are good reasons to promote critical thinking as a central educational goal!

Thinking critically about critical thinking

But we must also ask ourselves what forms of teaching and learning best serve God's mission in the world. I will not present a rigorous philosophical argument, but rather some suggestive observations generated during my years of living in the Majority World and thinking back on my Minority World education. I invite those who are better qualified to add rigor to what I can offer.

The issue of autonomy is a crucial starting point for reflecting Christianly on critical thinking. In many works on educational philosophy, the end goal of critical thinking is the development of the autonomous individual. Whether the desire for autonomy is a human universal need observed across cultures or something specific to more individualistic societies is a matter of considerable controversy.[10] Sadly, there has been insufficient theological assessment of whether autonomy should be seen as a human good, and discussion of the widespread emphasis on autonomy in critical thinking has not been particularly notable amongst Christian scholars. Rather, the main critique has come from secular feminist writers who have pressed

---

8   John Dewey, *How We Think: A Restatement of the Relation of Reflective Thinking to the Educative Process* (Boston: Heath and Co., 1933), 9.

9   Paulo Freire, *Pedagogy of the Oppressed* (New York: Continuum, 1970); Paulo Freire, *Pedagogy of Freedom: Ethics, Democracy and Civic Courage* (Lanham, MD: Rowman and Littlefield, 1998).

10 See for example Valery Chirkov, 'Culture, Personal Autonomy and Individualism: Their Relationships and Implications for Personal Growth and Well-Being', in *Perspectives and Progress in Contemporary Cross-Cultural Psychology: Proceedings from the 17th International Congress of the International Association for Cross-Cultural Psychology*, ed. Gang Zheng, Kwok Leung and John Adair (2008), https://worldca.org/yourls/ert452shaw1; Duane Rudy, Kennon Sheldon, Tsasha Awong and Hwee Hoon Tan, 'Autonomy, Culture, and Well-Being: The Benefits of Inclusive Autonomy', *Journal of Research in Personality* 41, no. 5 (2007): 983–1007.

for a greater relational emphasis in our educational paradigms, with one group coining the seemingly oxymoronic term 'relational autonomy'.[11]

Certainly, our unique individuality is a reflection of God's awesome creativity, but a desire for autonomy is a quite different matter. Was it not a desire for autonomy that catalysed the Fall? Autonomy literally means being a law unto oneself or having no master. I doubt that many of us want to train our students to be autonomous in the sense of making their own individual determination of rights as to what is right or ethical. Rather, our Trinitarian God has created us in the divine image as communal beings, and surely the divine imperative of love presses us to go beyond the autonomy of critical thinking to humble, quality reflection that respects others who form our community.

A focus on autonomous critical thinking tends to lead towards broad tolerance of other views, since everyone is entitled to their own opinion. Where there are no shared societal values, addressing foundational disagreements through common philosophical frameworks becomes impossible. Instead, all views are seen as legitimate and equally valid, and the imposition of one view over another is perceived as 'an action of violence'.[12] Tolerance of all other views is expected, unless someone's view is deemed harmful to society.

Tolerance is the only pathway by which an acutely individualized society can deal with the diversity of ideas generated by an approach to critical thinking that denies a place for community authority. But since any opposition to this type of tolerance is typically stigmatized as intolerant—and frankly, I don't know very many people who enjoy being seen as intolerant—many Christians, either consciously or unconsciously, have come to see tolerance as a Christian value.

Problems arise when groups differ as to what should be considered harmful to society. Muslims think gay advocacy should not be tolerated, whereas the gay community declares traditional views of sexuality bigoted. Some see voluntary euthanasia for the terminally ill as humanizing, whereas others see it as a dangerous precedent on the pathway to murdering people born with physical or intellectual challenges. With no way to negotiate these differences, so-called tolerance often morphs into efforts to silence competing voices. In Minority World societies today, the increasing emphasis on tolerance has been accompanied by increased censorship of divergent opinions—if not at the formal legal level, certainly through shaming on social media. Without a mooring in a transcendent reality, tolerance quickly devolves into a shouting war of all against all in the realm of discourse, in which the loudest voice seeks to silence dissenting voices.

---

11 See for example Catriona Mackenzie and Natalie Stoljar (eds.), *Relational Autonomy: Feminist Perspectives on Autonomy, Agency and the Social Self* (New York: Oxford University Press, 2000); Andrea Westlund, 'Rethinking Relational Autonomy', *Hypatia* 24, no. 4 (2009), 26-49; Holger Baumann, 'Reconsidering Relational Autonomy: Personal Autonomy for Socially Embedded and Temporally Extended Selves', *Analyse & Kritik* 30 (2008): 445-68.

12 The concept of metanarrative as violence is common in postmodern thought, notably in Jacques Derrida, *Of Grammatology*, trans. Gayatri Spivak (Baltimore, MD: Johns Hopkins University Press, 1967/2016), and Jean-François Lyotard, *The Postmodern Condition*, trans. Geoffrey Bennington and Brian Massumi (Manchester, UK: Manchester University Press, 1984).

Najla Kassab (now President of the World Communion of Reformed Churches) once commented to me, 'Critical thinking can lead to silence.' Tolerant, autonomous thinking may help us avoid being deceived by populist demagogues, but rational, critical, autonomous thinking without humility and love can divide and isolate individuals and destroy communities. Although correlation does not necessarily mean causation, it is noteworthy that with the increasing emphasis on autonomous thinking we have also witnessed growing societal fragmentation and escalating rates of divorce and suicide.

We should certainly urge respectfulness towards other views, but our primary Christian value should be love. Tolerance endures or puts up with others; love views others as fragile, damaged images of the living God who need to be cherished, and it embraces truth-telling as a way to healthy growth.

My wife loves me intensely, and part of her love entails her tolerance of my idiosyncratic behaviour patterns. But if she simply tolerates them, I cannot grow. I grow only when she gently and graciously points out the potential negative impact of those behaviours, helps me develop an action plan to produce change, and prays with me through its implementation. At the same time, I would never accept the criticism if I did not know her unconditional love for me. Love must precede critique.

How can we make love a stronger Christian paradigm than tolerance in our social relationships? The starting point is to build personal, caring relationships with those with whom we differ. Where personal contact is not possible, an empathetic reading of the other's story in context can help us view alternate perspectives with wisdom and grace.

Around the time of the 2019 Australian referendum on same-sex marriage, a prominent Christian woman began reaching out in love to a number of gay people she knew. When she was excoriated by the press for her opposition to same-sex marriage, one of these friends publicly defended her, saying, 'We disagree with her perspective, but you leave her alone. She loves us as real people, which is more than can be said for most of you journalists!'

Critical thinking is also generally touted as rational and logical. Again, since no one wants to be dismissed as irrational and illogical, we can too easily embrace an empiricist, autonomous stance as the primary end goal of our teaching. But biblical epistemology is always both holistic and relational.[13] It balances cognition with heart relationship and obedient action, going beyond 'faith seeking understanding' to 'faith seeking intelligent action'.[14] Jesus' great commandment (Mk 12:30) does not begin, 'Love the Lord your God with all your mind', but 'with all your heart', a perspective echoed in Paul's claim that justifying belief comes through the heart, not the mind (Rom 10:10). The broad biblical use of 'heart' to encompass thinking, feeling and acting points to a holistic and transformational understanding of learning and growth. To know God is to be changed by God, and this knowledge emerges in community. Indeed, to 'know' in the Scriptures is to have a relationship

---

13 Thomas Schirrmacher, 'Education and Learning in Christian Perspective', *Evangelical Review of Theology* 39, no. 2 (2015): 100–112.
14 Stephen Bevans, *Models of Contextual Theology* (Maryknoll, NY: Orbis, 2002), 73.

that finds its source in God's self-revelation to us. It is not a matter of us discovering truth, but of us coming to know *as we are already known* (1 Cor 13:12).[15]

This holistic understanding of learning and knowing pushes us to make biblical wisdom a prominent value. Paul emphasizes that Christian wisdom is not some form of abstract philosophizing, but a posture of humility and weakness before God, empowered by the Spirit (1 Cor 1:20–25; 2:6–14). Christian wisdom assumes the presence of a community within which we take rational and autonomous thinking seriously but also critique it. Within a community of wisdom, we can step back and see how some ideas can become problematic in practice. Christian wisdom goes beyond right thinking to right attitude and right action, and in this communal dance of thought, affect and practice broader nuances are realized that rationality alone fails to comprehend. Proverbs 3:5–6 advises us, 'The fear of the Lord is the beginning of wisdom.' Being renewed through this wisdom can provide a much-needed lens for assessing rational critical thinking and for promoting the common good. Only wisdom can provide guidance towards a fruitful life, one enriched by relationships and meaning.

Paul was profoundly concerned that Christians not be conformed to the patterns of the surrounding society, but the alternative to conformity was not 'think for yourself'. Rather, it was a call to 'be transformed by the renewing of the mind, so that you may test what is the will of God—what is good and acceptable and perfect' (Rom 12:2). Some Christian scholars have seen in Paul's reference to 'renewing of your mind' some sort of biblical justification for autonomous, rational, critical thinking. However, a careful exegesis finds that Paul's priority is not the establishment of a personal intellectual perspective but an active, obedient response to the will of God. The term he uses here, *dokimazein*, suggests not intellectual analysis but the ability to 'test' or 'prove' experientially what is God's will. Later in Romans 12, Paul speaks about humility, spiritual gifts in the body of Christ, and wisdom for Christian living, indicating further that the renewing of one's mind should be demonstrated in changed attitudes and obedient action. Gerhard Maier captured this message: 'A critical method [in interpreting Scripture] must fail, because it presents an inner impossibility. For the correlative or counterpart to revelation is not critique but obedience; it is not correction … but it is a let-me-be-corrected.'[16]

From individual, critical thinking to collective, constructive thinking

The unspoken assumption that autonomous critical thinking is the measure of quality work has been exported around the globe, especially where educational agendas have been shaped by Minority World accreditation systems or (worse) when Majority World colleges are led by white Minority World males. I sometimes wonder whether the normative expectation of autonomous critical thinking carries

---

15 Relational knowledge forms the epistemological foundation for Parker Palmer's seminal educational text, *To Know as We Are Known: A Spirituality of Education* (San Francisco, CA: Harper & Row, 1983).
16 Gerhard Maier, *The End of the Historical-Critical Method*, trans. Edwin Leverenz and Rudolph Norden (St. Louis, MO: Concordia, 1977), 23.

overtones of neo-colonial cultural imperialism.[17] It is a decidedly Minority World notion with a heritage deeply rooted in Greek philosophy and atomistic individualism, a heritage that is not shared globally,[18] and one that has generated highly problematic outcomes in many parts of the world.[19]

In his seminal work on intercultural rhetoric, Robert Kaplan[20] offers a set of foundational questions that influence patterns of discussion and argument in different cultural contexts:

1. *What may be discussed?* What sorts of limitations are there on acceptable and unacceptable topics of discussion and research? In some settings, the limitations may be related to social concerns, whereas other settings may define how narrow or broad a discussion topic should be.

2. *Who has the authority to speak or write?* In what ways do social, political and religious authority structures influence the shape and content of what is talked about or studied?

3. *What form(s) may the writing take?* To what extent are the rhetorical patterns of surrounding cultures allowed to influence the forms in which students write?

4. *What is evidence?* Minority World patterns of linear, empiricist, logical argumentation can be offensive and distasteful in societies that place greater value on life experience, wisdom and story.

5. *What arrangement of evidence is likely to appeal (be convincing) to readers?* To what extent is argumentation expected to be explicit in students' presentation of their work, or are implicit approaches preferred?

The answers to these questions are profoundly shaped by culture, and what constitutes good reasoning varies across contexts.[21] A wide variety of interpretative frameworks can make good sense of the world, and each is based on a different set

---

17 Ladislaus Semali and Joe Kincheloe, *What Is Indigenous Knowledge? Voices from the Academy* (Milton Park, UK: Taylor and Francis, 1999), 31; Sharan Merriam, 'An Introduction to Non-Western Perspectives on Learning and Knowing', in Sharan Merriam and Associates, *Non-Western Perspectives on Learning and Knowing* (Malabar, FL: Krueger, 2007), 1–20; Sandra Egege and Salah Kutieleh, 'Critical Thinking: Teaching Foreign Notions to Foreign Students', *International Education Journal* 4, no. 4 (2004), 75–85.
18 See for example Jie-Qi Chen, 'China's Assimilation of MI Theory in Education', in *Multiple Intelligences around the World*, ed. Jie-Qi Chen, Seana Moran and Howard Gardner (San Francisco, CA: Jossey-Bass, 2009), 29–42.
19 See various articles in Shaw and Dharamraj, *Challenging Tradition*.
20 Robert Kaplan, 'Foreword', in *Contrastive Rhetoric Revisited and Redefined*, ed. Clayann Panetta (New York, NY: Routledge, 2008), ix.
21 Jonathan Ichikawa and Matthias Steup, 'The Analysis of Knowledge', in *The Stanford Encyclopedia of Philosophy* (Summer 2018 ed.), ed. Edward Zalta, https://worldea.org/yourls/ert452shaw2; Stephen Stich and Richard Nisbett, 'Justification and the Psychology of Human Reasoning', in *Collected Papers*, vol. 2: *Knowledge, Rationality, and Morality, 1978–2010*, ed. Stephen Stich (Oxford, UK: Oxford University Press, 2012), 36–48; Jonathan Weinberg, Shaun Nichols and Stephen Stich, 'Normativity and Epistemic Intuitions', *Philosophical Topics* 29 (2001): 429–60.

of assumptions.²² In particular, I have been struck by the fundamentally different understandings of the first two questions between collectivist and individualistic societies. In more individualistic societies, such as Australia and the United States, the normative assumption is that we should promote students' development of a strongly autonomous voice. We encourage students to speak with confidence, question assumptions and challenge those in authority, without reference to their relationship to the broader community. In most parts of the world, such individualistic assumptions would be seen as disrespectful, divisive and destabilizing.²³

Collectivist societies begin with an understanding that the young need to see older people as a great source of deep wisdom. This stands in stark contrast to the dominant narrative often delivered to young people in the Minority World, where aging means increasing irrelevance. A pervasive assumption in the Middle East, Africa, Asia and elsewhere is that young adults does not have the maturity to speak with authority. They should first spend time learning from the elders, and perhaps at a later time their experience and quality of life will earn them the right to speak authoritatively.

When teaching in Beirut, I initially reacted negatively to the notable emphasis on rote learning. With some ethnocentric arrogance, I viewed the local education systems in the Middle East, Africa and large swathes of Asia as backward and destructive, even as contributing to the rise of authoritarian dictatorships. Over time, however, I gained a more nuanced appreciation of local learning approaches. Given these societies' assumptions about how younger people should learn the accumulated wisdom of their elders, a focus on rote learning makes more sense. Students begin by learning and embracing the perspective of those who have acquired wisdom over long experience.²⁴ The opinions of the young are rarely taken seriously, even when they are better educated than their elders.

Comparable patterns appear in much of the Majority World. For example, in a study of self-directed learning in the Korean context (a context greatly influenced by Confucianism), most Minority World educational values were seen as inappropriate. Rather, 'a person becoming independent of his or her parents, teachers or other people tends to be considered threatening [to] the stability of a community he or she belongs to. ... Becoming independent without being

---

22   William Merrifield, *Culture and Critical Thinking: Exploring Culturally Informed Reasoning Processes in a Lebanese University* (PhD dissertation, George Fox University, 2018), 12.
23   Black, 'Scholarship in Our Own Words'.
24   In much of the world, the dominant learning culture follows the master–disciple approach, as opposed to the independent learning approach promoted in European-influenced education systems. See for example Lal Senanayake, 'The Imperative of Cultural Integration in Advanced Theological Studies: Perspectives from the Majority World', in Shaw and Dharamraj, *Challenging Tradition*, 109–26. Margaret Kumar has observed that moving from a more collectivist master–disciple model to an independent learning approach is one of the major challenges facing international students who come to Australia. See Kumar, 'International Candidates' Transition to a "Doctorate Downunder"', in *Doctorates Downunder: Keys to Successful Doctoral Study in Australia and Aotearoa New Zealand*, ed. Carey Denholm and Terry Evans (Camberwell, Australia: ACER, 2012), 155.

interdependent passes for immaturity or self-centeredness.'[25]

The implications for higher education are profound. Kaplan observes, 'In the United States composition tradition, anyone—even a lowly student—has the authority to write and to hold and express an opinion, but in more traditional cultures, the young have no such authority.' Kaplan suggests this may be a major reason why such students quote published sources extensively rather than offering more independent insights. These students are often 'accused of failing to exercise critical thinking, but they may not see themselves as authorized to undertake such an act.'[26]

In observing highly collectivist societies first-hand, I have realized that healthy multigenerational communities cannot function without a strong sense of authority, respect for elders and a focus on wisdom. The idea that all opinions have the right to be spoken compromises the overall quality of conversations within the community.

We can learn much from the African concept of *ubuntu*, which is foundational to traditional African educational philosophy and practice. *Ubuntu* expresses concern for human welfare in the context of community, as I affirm my own humanity by recognizing the humanity of others: 'I am because you are.' The purpose of education then becomes focused less on developing an autonomous individual voice and more on the development of virtues such as kindness, generosity, compassion, benevolence, courtesy, and respect and concern for others.[27]

Although the students I taught in Beirut came from collectivist, deferential societies, they were also being educated to assume significant Christian leadership roles. Consequently, they needed to move from rote learning to developing a meaningful and well-informed voice so that they could work productively and be listened to in their communities, while still honouring and respecting the existing leadership of their communities. My colleagues and I at the Arab Baptist Theological Seminary (ABTS) also sensed a need to develop in our students the ethical commitment to challenge leadership that is corrupt, dishonest and abusive. But such a voice must be constantly tempered by respect and an element of submission, lest our students be perceived as openly criticizing their elders and thus ignored. To be heard, they needed to speak constructively within a respectful relationship with the leaders and the wider community.

Finding the balance between a voice that acknowledges its own limited maturity and life experience and speaking up to provide quality leadership is a challenging teaching assignment. But after seeing our graduates in action and speaking with people in their communities, we believe that ABTS has made progress in addressing this challenge. In a faculty discussion in February 2018, we identified the following

---

25 Yoonkyeong Nah, 'Can a Self-Directed Learner Be Independent, Autonomous and Interdependent? Implications for Practice', *Adult Learning* 11, no. 1 (1999), 18–25. Compare to Sheila Fabiano, *Perceptions of Instituto Superior De Teologia Evangélica No Lubango Graduates in Angola: Implications for Theological Education in Learning and Ministry Practice* (PhD dissertation, Trinity International University, 2015), 12–27.
26 Kaplan, 'Foreword', x.
27 Philip Higgs, 'Towards an Indigenous African Educational Discourse: A Philosophical Reflection', *International Review of Education* 54 (2008): 445–58.

processes that have helped our students develop a clear and respectful voice in their community:

- The teacher's perspective is crucial. Students in collectivist societies defer to authority, but authority is easily abused. When students show respect for authority, it is easy for a teacher to take advantage of that respect and not return it in full measure to the students. Concerned about the arrogance and power differential that authority figures often exude, we emphasized that our teachers must speak with both humility and confidence. Modelling good listening was a key. Also significant were actions that evidenced an attitude of service to the students, even as simple as picking up a book that a student had dropped—acts that would not normally take place in their home contexts, but which demonstrated pathways to servanthood in leadership.
- We also encouraged students to challenge one another graciously and to demonstrate how they could do so with respect and humility. We wanted our students to become equipped to respectfully challenge abusive power dynamics wherever they exist. We looked for opportunities to train students in constructive and meaningful critique. Being a theological college, we had daily chapel gatherings, which we asked the students to lead. Several times a week, the student leaders and chapel speakers were critiqued publicly by fellow students and privately by individual professors. Placing students in the position of teaching their professors was counter-cultural and intimidating, but it helped them build confidence and develop their voices.
- Shifting from lecture to small-group discussion became a model for an alternate form of leadership and decision-making for our students. However, rather than individual students sharing their own personal perspective, summaries of each group's discussions were shared by a group spokesperson. Being the spokesperson for a group gave students the opportunity to practice finding a voice that speaks respectfully on behalf of their community.
- Likewise, we promoted the use of group projects rather than individual assessments, recognizing that a significant part of our desired hidden curriculum was to develop the ability to work together towards a common goal, rather than in competition with one another.[28] Working collaboratively both respected the collective nature of the society our students came from and encouraged the development of their individual voices.
- We structured our policies and official communications formationally rather than legislatively. For example, the academic integrity policy at ABTS begins with a narrative acknowledging the difficulty of moving from a rote learning culture to one that expects students to develop a personal voice while also showing respect for existing experts. When students break the policy, processes are step-by-step and pastoral, recognizing that the pathway to integrity is a long journey.

---

28 Perry Shaw, *Transforming Theological Education: A Practical Handbook for Integrative Learning* (Carlisle, UK: Langham, 2014), 79–92.

Practical implications

There is a widespread perception that 'the West knows best and tells the rest', but the time has come for a level of reciprocity as together we learn from one another through the richness of the global church. Surely, developing a constructive, respectful voice in one's community should be central not just to theological education in more collectivist societies, but even in more individualist cultural contexts such as Australia, North America or Europe—and all the more so as the proportion of non-Anglo membership grows in many Minority World churches.

At ABTS, our students had been trained not to speak and we needed to help them develop a respectful but thoughtful voice. Many Minority World educators face the opposite challenge of welcoming students who have been socialized by the broader educational and social environment to say what they think, not always with reason or respect. Here are a few suggestions, many of which I have already seen practised in Minority World schools, but which need further development.

- Students should be encouraged to speak more tentatively, understanding how much they have yet to learn and that wisdom comes with life experience. A loss of intergenerational respect can be a major deficiency in many students' learning. One useful exercise may be to ask students to share a research paper or even classroom notes with an older person in the community. The elder would be invited to evaluate the student in terms of both the clarity of the content and the respect he or she has exhibited.
- Approach class participation with more caution. We assume that when students make comments and express their opinions and ideas, this is a sign of engagement. Indeed, it may be. However, these opinions are often expressed without concern about whether they make sense, whether the opinion has evidence to support it, or what impact the idea might have on the wider community. Having students first discuss their ideas in small groups or even in pairs can improve the calibre of their comments and the tone in which they are presented.
- Move away from a debate mentality, with students trying to win the argument, towards working in diverse teams to develop win-win solutions that serve the whole community. The education literature is recognizing that the information revolution, particularly social media, has not led to the original utopian hope of greater mutual understanding, but rather to greater polarization, antagonism and the development of echo chambers.[29] A debate mentality fosters the toxic nature of much of what we now see on social media platforms such as Facebook and Twitter, with many people (even Christian leaders) seeing these platforms as an opportunity for unexpurgated criticism of those with whom they disagree. I wonder whether our emphasis on critical rather than constructive thinking feeds

---

29 See for example Ed Stetzer and Andrew MacDonald, 'How Can and Should We Reach and Train Our Future Pastors and Christian Leaders?' *Christian Education Journal* 17, no. 1 (2020): 160–76; Greg Lukianoff and Jonathan Haidt, *The Coddling of the American Mind: How Good Intentions and Bad Ideas Are Setting Up a Generation for Failure* (New York: Penguin, 2018), 131.

into such postures. The contemporary technological environment makes it even more imperative for teachers and students to consider the impact their personal words and actions have on the wider community.
- The use of case studies and problem-based learning as a basis for stimulating and developing reflective judgement can stimulate high-quality, multi-dimensional reflection.[30] When these approaches are structured as a group exercise, the end goal becomes not so much individual critical thinking but collective resolution of problems. Having students discuss essay or research tasks in groups before tackling them individually, or having students work jointly on written tasks, promotes teamwork, collaboration and potentially a gentler voice."
- Speak the truth with love (Eph 4:15). Although the principle of developing genuine care and respectful speech is applicable to any classroom, those involved in theological education should especially embrace these words. This requires restraint and wisdom along with courage. Our own practices as teachers can model truth in love, as can the behaviours we require from our students.

Some of the key contrasts between critical and constructive thinking are summarized in the table below.

Critical Thinking	Constructive Thinking
Individual and autonomous	Collaborative and collective
Primarily cognitive dimension of learning	Engages cognitive, affective and behavioural dimensions of learning
Emphasis on rationality	Emphasis on wisdom, obedience and the good of the community
Accountability is to self and the academy based on individual assessment	Accountability is to the community based on broad intergenerational assessment
Deconstructive without a requirement for reconstruction	Includes deconstruction, but critique is unacceptable without constructive alternative
From above	From below
Danger of pride and self-righteousness	Danger of blind acceptance of evil

Conclusion

I hope that as you encounter the term 'critical thinking' in the future, you will think twice and perhaps consider how constructive thinking may be a richer alternative. I further urge Majority World educational leaders to be cautious about adopting Minority World educational perspectives and instead to seek local models that may better nurture holistic and contextually significant teaching and learning and thus more effectively serve God's mission in this world.

---

30 Patricia King and Karen Kitchener, *Developing Reflective Judgment: Understanding and Promoting Intellectual Growth and Critical Thinking in Adolescents and Adults* (San Francisco, CA: Jossey-Bass, 1994), 147; John Jusu, 'Problem-Based Learning in Advanced Theological Studies', in Shaw and Dharamraj, eds., *Challenging Tradition*, 209–31.

Can We Not Mourn with Those Who Mourn?

Walter Riggans

The book of Psalms is full of laments, but our church services today are overwhelmingly dominated by praise songs. Why the difference? This article examines the problem, calls for a song selection that opens its arms to the suffering, and offers some powerful, positive modern examples.

The place of hymnody in the life of the church should be to enable us to worship God in all his fulness, as we come before him in all our fulness. Unfortunately, I find that even though pastorally our hearts are readily warm to one another when we see brothers and sisters in distress, there is often a coolness between us when we sing together in worship.

One reason for this problem is that much of our hymnody today, especially what we commonly call 'Christian songs', is at risk of losing a highly significant aspect of our fulness in worship—namely, our ability to deal with those times when life is terribly hard and faith is a genuine struggle. Are these not also times when worship is appropriate? Should we not be able to embrace one another in the solidarity of sadness and loss as well as in times of joy and spontaneity?

I will use the Psalter, where distress is fully addressed, as my benchmark for singing in worship that reflects the fulness of life with God. Many Christians and church traditions have incorporated the Psalms into liturgy and Christian life in various ways, not limited to hymnody. As Walter Brueggeman has stated:

> The hold that the Psalms have on the contemporary practice of faith and piety … is evident liturgically with regular and sustained use of the Psalms in the daily office, generation after generation. It is evident devotionally in those free church traditions which are not so keen on liturgical use but which nurture persons in their own prayer life to draw guidance and strength from the Psalms. And thirdly, contemporary use is evident pastorally, for many pastors find in the Psalms the most remarkable and reliable resources for many situations.[1]

I have worshipped in many churches, from a wide range of theological and liturgical traditions. Although there are exceptions, generally our worship reflects a

---

Walter Riggans (PhD, University of Birmingham) is the Learning and Development Manager of the Congregational Federation and the Director of Studies of its ministerial training course. This article is based on a paper he presented in 2017 at the Moravian Church and School at Fulneck, UK, as part of an event celebrating the 500th anniversary of the Reformation.

---

1 Walter A. Brueggeman, *The Psalms and the Life of Faith* (Minneapolis, MN: Fortress, 1995), 6–7.

strange coolness about spending quality time and space alongside sisters and brothers who are experiencing serious pain. Our practice can imply that we consider it exceptional for any Christian to undergo severe sorrow. Moreover, where people are suffering, our practice implies that they should simply sublimate their sorrows and pain and join with other believers in praise.

We seem to assume that there will never be more than one or two in a church service whose heart is breaking. Because of this assumption, many consider that it would be disproportionate and inappropriate to recognize and welcome, in our corporate worship, those who are living through such an experience.

We are not cool to one another in our wider relationships, with regard to acknowledging each other's grief, fear and doubt. Pastors visit their congregants personally, pray with and for them, mourn with those who mourn, and find practical ways to help. Yet when we gather in worship services, we rarely pause to mourn with the mourning; to visit liturgically with those who are afraid; or to sing with those who doubt, grieve or are angry with God—and who often feel further guilt and shame because of those feelings.

The Psalms are an intentional, canonical book

Scholars today tend to regard the Psalter as a unified book, a canonical whole.[2] For most of the twentieth century, it was treated as a collection of isolated works, but the growing consensus now is that the canonical Psalter was intentional, albeit with differences among scholars as to the meta-theme(s).[3]

The book of Psalms is often described as the hymnbook of Israel, or of the second temple.[4] As Israel sang (and still sings) these Psalms, they learned (and still learn) who God is and how to relate to him in the full gamut of life's experiences. The Psalms, in all their fulness, frame the worship of the Jewish people to this day. Our hymnals and songbooks should reflect and express that same holistic life within the Church. The Psalter should be not only our inspiration but also our benchmark.

Hymns and songs teach theology

In the nineteeenth century, Congregational minister R. W. Dale wrote, 'Let me write the hymns of a Church and I care not who writes the theology.'[5] His point is sound, and scholars and practitioners alike have recognized it as a genuine insight. A generation ago, two hymnologists affirmed Dale's observation, stating, 'The basic beliefs of most Christians have been formulated more by the hymns they sing than

---

2   See the comments of Roger Whybray in John Day, Robert P. Gordon and H. G. M. Williamson (eds.), *Wisdom in Ancient Israel: Essays in Honour of J. A. Emerton* (Cambridge: Cambridge University Press, 1995), 155.
3   See Gerald Wilson, 'The Shape of the Book of Psalms', *Interpretation* 46 (1992): 129–42; David M. Howard Jr., 'Recent Trends in Psalms Study', in David W. Baker, *The Face of Old Testament Studies: A Study of Contemporary Approaches* (Grand Rapids: Baker, 1999), 332–33.
4   For example, Norman K. Gottwald, *The Hebrew Bible: A Socio-Literary Introduction* (Philadelphia: Fortress, 1995), 525.
5   Quoted in Ian Bradley, *Abide with Me: The World of Victorian Hymns* (London, SCM, 1997), 81.

by the preaching they hear or the Bible study they pursue.'[6] And in 1998, Michael Jinkins noted, 'We cannot expect a people's understanding of God to reach much higher than their hymn books.'[7]

It is therefore crucial to ensure that the theology taught in our hymns and songs addresses the whole of life lived under and for God. Throughout church history, hymn writers have recognized the value of hymns in teaching theology to the church. Martin Luther revived the early church's practice of giving prominence to corporate hymn singing in worship services. He composed original texts and translated other texts to create a body of hymnody that not only encouraged praise but also instructed worshippers in Christian doctrine.

In 1780, *A Collection of Hymns for the Use of the People Called Methodists* was published. John Wesley viewed this book as a summation of the central doctrines of Methodism. He stated in its preface that the collection was 'large enough to contain all the important truths of our most holy religion, whether speculative or practical; yea, to illustrate them all, and to prove them both by Scripture and reason'.[8]

This hymnal addressed the full range of Christian doctrine, from prevenient grace to Christian perfection. However, it was also intended to deal with the full range of Christian experience in life. Wesley noted, 'The hymns are not carelessly jumbled together, but carefully ranged under their proper heads, according to the experiences of real Christians. So this book is in effect a little body of experimental and practical divinity.'[9]

Note Wesley's deliberate reference to the experiences of 'real Christians'. This was no idealized canon of hymns for an idealized church. Rather, the purpose was to disseminate a fully comprehensive theology to the widest possible audience. A strong, fully biblical hymnody is so important for the life and health of the church. But such a hymnody needs to embrace the full range of the Psalter's expression of worship and honest relationship with God.

The Psalter is far more than praise, and our hymnals and song books should be too

We need our hymnody to embrace us in the fulness of our lives—mourning as well as rejoicing. Once again, Brueggemann has captured this for us:

> The book of Psalms provides the most reliable theological, pastoral, and liturgical resource given to us in the biblical tradition. In season and out of season, generation after generation, faithful women and men turn to the Psalms as a most helpful resource for conversation with God about things that matter

---

6   Harry Eskew and Hugh T. McElrath, *Sing with Understanding* (Nashville, TN: Broadman, 1980), 59.
7   Michael Jinkins, *In the House of the Lord: Inhabiting the Psalms of Lament* (Collegeville, MN: Liturgical Press, 1998), 34.
8   See the edition by Kevin Twit, *Preface and Table of Contents of 1780 Hymn Book* (n.d.), paragraph 4, https://worldea.org/yourls/ert452riggans1.
9   Twit, *Preface and Table of Contents*, paragraph 4.

most. The Psalms are helpful because they are a genuinely dialogical literature that expresses both sides of the conversation of faith.[10]

In the Jewish structure of the Hebrew Bible, the Psalter is the lead book in the third of three groupings of books. We have the Torah (five books of Moses), the Nevi'im (former and latter Prophets), and then the Ketuvim (other Writings). Appreciating the theological importance of the Psalter's positioning at the head of this third grouping, Paul House describes it as 'a perfect book to begin the Writings'. What brings him to this conclusion? 'Psalms probes the depths of suffering and discusses the origins and applications of wisdom, topics that occupy Job and Proverbs, the next two books in the canon.'[11]

Hermann Gunkel's seminal work on the different genres of psalms has been developed, challenged and refined since the 1920s. However, his insights into form-critical categories changed the study of Psalms forever.[12] In spite of differences in theological framework and spiritual nuance, there is still a consensus that the Psalter contains distinct genres, reflecting a range of experiences that the writers bring to worship.

Gunkel placed a large number of the psalms in the genre of 'lament'. Those who view the Psalter differently from Gunkel still acknowledge the significance of the laments as an important component of Israel's worship.

Brueggemann has been influential in redirecting understandings of how to categorize Psalms. In his interaction with Gunkel's work, he introduced a three-fold typology:

- 'orientation': the absence of tension, the celebration of the created order, divine retribution, blessing;
- 'disorientation': lament, doubt, pain;
- 'reorientation': renewed confidence in God, thanksgiving and praise.[13]

This paradigm recognizes the prominence of the 'disorientation' category within the Psalter. As R. W. L. Moberly affirms, even though the Hebrew name for the book of Psalms is *Tehillim* (Praises) and the book ends with a series of psalms that all conclude with *hallelu-Yah* (Praise the Lord!), the single most common feature in Psalms is the lament.[14] Depending on how you categorize the psalms and whether you weight them by length, somewhere between one-third and one-half of the Psalter consists of individual and communal laments, or of psalms in which laments play a part.[15] This is a staggering percentage.

---

10 Walter A. Brueggemann, *The Message of the Psalms* (Minneapolis, MN: Augsburg, 1984), 15.
11 Paul R. House, *Old Testament Theology* (Downers Grove, IL: IVP Academic, 1998), 402.
12 For a good summary of recent trends, see Howard, *Recent Trends*, 360–65. John J. Collins presents a useful table of classifications of the Psalms in his *Introduction to the Hebrew Bible* (Minneapolis, MN: Fortress, 2004), 469.
13 Brueggemann, *Message of the Psalms*, 20–21.
14 R. W. L. Moberly, *Old Testament Theology: Reading the Hebrew Bible as Christian Scripture* (Grand Rapids: Baker Academic, 2013), 211.
15 Joyce A. Zimmerman, *Worship with Gladness: Understanding Worship from the Heart* (Grand Rapids: Eerdmans, 2014), 70, regards the laments as comprising almost half the Psalms.

In light of this, John Comer wonders why we are not more honest with God in our Christian worship. Not only would doing so more fully represent us as real Christians, but it would have more biblical integrity.[16] Anyone who doubts the importance of the psalms of lament should consider their role in Jesus' life. In the gospels, we find Jesus' passion narrated with frequent references to these laments, especially Psalms 22, 31, 69 and 88.[17]

The laments confirm to us that our anxieties, doubts, and sense of loss and grief, even anger at what God seems to have allowed in our lives, all have a place within our worship of God—corporately as well as privately. These realities of our lives are not condemned in Scripture, nor are they hidden away in an embarrassed corner of the canon. Instead, they are out in the open and presented as if they are entitled to be there, as indeed they are. Human struggle is prominent in the Old Testament books of Job, Ecclesiastes, Jeremiah and Lamentations as well as Psalms.

David Firth regards the Psalter as a paradox that we need to appreciate and embrace. He explains the paradox as follows:

> A book that contains so much that is dark, so much that represents the real struggles of God's people to understand what it means to be faithful and how it is that God is in turn faithful to them, is also fundamentally a book of praises. … It is precisely because the Psalms bring these two elements together in their record of prayers offered to God that they continue to be a source of comfort to so many believers.[18]

The Psalter expresses our lives in their full range of experience. Martin Luther wrote:

> Where does one find finer words of joy than in the psalms of praise and thanksgiving? There you look into the hearts of all the saints, as into fair and pleasant gardens, yes, as into heaven itself. There you see what fine and pleasant flowers of the heart spring up from all sorts of fair and happy thoughts toward God, because of his blessings. On the other hand, where do you find deeper, more sorrowful, more pitiful words of sadness than in the psalms of lamentation? There again you look into the hearts of all the saints, as into death, yes, as into hell itself. … Hence it is that the Psalter is the book of all saints; and everyone, in whatever situation he may be, finds in that situation psalms and words that fit his ease, that suit him as if they were put there just for his sake, so that he could not put it better himself, or find or wish for anything better.[19]

John Calvin wrote in his commentary:

> There is not an emotion of which anyone can be conscious that is not here represented as in a mirror. Or rather, the Holy Spirit has here drawn to life all

---

16 John M. Comer, *Garden City: Work, Rest, and the Art of Being Human* (Grand Rapids: Zondervan, 2015).
17 See Rebekah Eklund, *Jesus Wept. The Significance of Jesus' Laments in the New Testament* (London. Bloomsbury T&T Clark, 2015).
18 David G. Firth, *Hear, O Lord: A Spirituality of the Psalms* (Derbyshire, UK: Cliff College Publishing, 2005), 3.
19 Jaroslav J. Pelikan et al. (eds.), *Luther's Works*, vol. 35: *Word and Sacrament I* (Philadelphia: Fortress, 1999), 254–57.

the griefs, sorrows, fears, doubts, hopes, cares, perplexities, in short, all distracting emotions with which the minds of men are wont to be agitated.[20]

Even the so-called 'imprecatory' Psalms, though we may consider them to be 'harsh, childish, or "primitive"',[21] were not said in private, in whispers or in shame. They became part of the public worship of the people of God, gathered as one before God.[22]

Doctrinal compliance is not the same as faith formation

Christians in liturgical churches are far more keenly aware than those from other traditions that faith development involves much more than learning and adhering to orthodox doctrine. But because song writers realize that hymns are an effective teaching medium for Christians, some of them tend to focus on what is considered a sound approach to doctrine. Hymns can be used rhetorically to reinforce what we are supposed to believe theologically.

But God does not always intervene in life's difficult circumstances, and it is not always easy to align our faith with our doctrinal aspirations. In times of distress, we turn for help to the Psalms, because so many of them identify with our despair and confusion. Grant Osborne writes concerning the spirituality of the Psalms:

> Primarily, the psalms center on worship and prayer; they demonstrate better than any other biblical genre Israel's God-consciousness. They make no actual theological statements, but their very God-centeredness is highly theological. Every area of life is related to God, and he is seen as sovereign over all.[23]

Can our church hymnodies serve us just as well in our honest, postmodern lives? Hymnody should not be just about praise or about teaching theology, but also about forming *faith*—and not only for new Christians, but for all of us at our various stages of Christian maturity. Our corporate worship, including our singing, has a significant role to play in this process. The key question is how we can effectively integrate our struggles with the difficulties of life, as well as our joys, into our hymns and songs.

Reflecting both his scholarship and his experience of the serious difficulties that have faced Christians in the Philippines over the decades, Federico Villanueva insists that we must face up to the challenge of the laments in the Psalms. He writes in the introduction to his commentary:

---

20 John Calvin, *Commentary on the Book of Psalms*, trans. J. Anderson (Grand Rapids: Eerdmans, 1949), xxxvi–xxxvii.

21 Gerald T. Sheppard, '"Enemies" and the Politics of Prayer in the Book of Psalms', in *The Bible and Liberation: Political and Social Hermeneutics*, ed. Norman K. Gottwald and Richard A. Horsley, rev. ed. (London: SPCK, 1993), 377.

22 For a rumination on the contemporary use of the imprecatory psalms, see John Goldingay and Kathleen S. Goldingay, 'The Sting in the Psalms, Part 2', *Theology* 118, no. 1 (2015): 3–9. A controversial argument for reaffirming the place of the imprecatory psalms in the church is provided by Jace Broadhurst, 'Should Cursing Continue? An Argument for Imprecatory Psalms in Biblical Theology', *Africa Journal of Evangelical Theology* 23, no. 1 (2004): 61–89.

23 Grant R. Osborne, *The Hermeneutical Spiral. A Comprehensive Introduction to Biblical Interpretation* (Downers Grove, IL: IVP Academic, 2006), 237.

Although Psalms was called the Book of Praises ... there are more psalms of lament than psalms of praise. ... Although many of the lament psalms contain praise or move to praise at the end, still the space given to lament in these psalms is remarkable. ... Those who put the book together ... knew through their own experience that the road to the land of praise leads through fields of lament.[24]

If our hymnody addresses serious suffering with only brief summary references, advancing as quickly as possible to the goodness or power of God and urging the sufferer to immediately commence praising and thanking God, then, apart from not really ministering to the person in need, we are also in danger of teaching a cheap grace. Discipleship can be costly, and an easy Christian life is not guaranteed to true disciples. Whether or not we would go as far as Bonhoeffer in holding that this cheap grace is a 'deadly enemy of the Church',[25] we should surely agree that it is counter-productive to faith formation and less than fully biblical.

Christian hymnody contains some of the most tightly packed, concise doctrinal and devotional thought of the church.[26] Through congregational song, God's people learn their language about God, as well as how to speak with God. Songs of worship shape our journey of faith. Is there sufficient pastoral breadth in our hymnody? Do we sing songs that are appropriate to the many life situations in which Christians find themselves? In the middle of the last century, André Chouraqui famously wrote about the Psalter:

> We were born with this book in our very bones. A small book: 150 poems; 150 steps between death and life; 150 mirrors of our rebellions and our loyalties, of our agonies and our resurrections.[27]

Some 65 years later, one characteristic of our postmodern age is that even within the churches, there is a desire, even a demand, for acceptance of the doubts and fears in our lives. Christians know about agony as well as resurrection in life, and it is increasingly a mark of postmodern Christian life to insist on holistic, personal authenticity in worship.[28]

Take time to mourn with those who mourn

Romans 12:15, 'Mourn with those who mourn', is a key verse in this context. We should not try too soon, or with too much acceleration, to move suffering people on theologically, spiritually and emotionally. Yet that is what so many worship leaders and writers on the subject of worship seem to do. And this attitude pervades contemporary Christian song writing.

We need to take a lesson from Job's friends. Although they subsequently try to convince Job to accept an understanding of his plight that Job knows is not appropriate, and even though God reprimands them at the end of the book for not

---

24 Federico G. Villanueva, *Psalms 1-72* (Carlisle, UK: Langham Partnership, 2016), 2.
25 Dietrich Bonhoeffer, *The Cost of Discipleship* (London: SCM Press, 2001), 3.
26 Harold M. Best, *Music Through the Eyes of Faith* (San Francisco, CA: Harper, 1993), 200.
27 N. A. Chouraqui, *Les Psaumes* (Paris: Presses Universitaires de France, 1956), 1.
28 See Stuart Murray, *Church after Christendom* (Waynesboro, GA: Paternoster Press, 2005); Christian Smith and Patricia Snell, *Souls in Transition: The Religious Lives of Emerging Adults in America* (New York: Oxford University Press, 2009).

speaking rightly about him, they begin the right way—weeping with Job and sitting on the ground with this devastated man for seven days and nights, without saying a word, 'because they saw how great his suffering was' (Job 2:12–13).

We should not trust any teaching about Christian worship that does not seriously tackle the aspects of life covered by the category of 'lament'. For example, one popular British book which has been influential with church and worship leaders, and which sets out to present the biblical foundations of Christian worship, completely overlooks this dimension.[29]

A more recent American example is a book by a widely read pastor and Christian songwriter which purports to offer high-level guidance about worship, including our hymns and songs.[30] Within it, six very brief passages mention the realities of doubt, despair or grief in our lives. In each case, the author moves on swiftly from these brief mentions to the 'solution' of praising God. There is no discussion of pastoral fellowship with someone who is suffering, no consideration of pausing in song to allow expressions of anger or sorrow to God as we bring our honest selves to him.

At one point, the writer seems to belittle the need for mature, pastoral concern for our brothers and sisters in a public worship setting:

> Probably one of the greatest challenges we face in the church is distractions. It's enough to be distracted internally by … pains and anxieties. But distractions can also be external. There might be a loud, musically deficient vocalist right behind you.[31]

To classify a struggle with cancer, divorce or sudden unemployment as a 'distraction' is to betray the integrity of the Psalter and true worship.

Much of what is written today about hymnody and worship strikes me as shallow triumphalism. We need depth in our worship, finding support to live with God at the heart of our life of faith, knowing that we do not need to look for resolution elsewhere.[32] As Kathleen Billman and Daniel Migliore contend:

> The prayer of lament, or what might also be called the prayer of pain and protest, is vital to theology and pastoral ministry today … it is a profound resource for personal and corporate healing, and … it is inseparably related to the capacity of hope and praise. Without the resistance and protest that are expressed in the prayer of lament, Christian life, worship, and ministry can quickly become shallow and evasive.[33]

Similarly, Joyce Zimmerman points out that the complaints that we find in the laments seldom end without any sense of moving forward with God. 'The lament brings about a transformation in the individual or community', she observes.[34]

---

29 Susan J. White, *Groundwork of Christian Worship* (Peterborough, UK: Epworth Press, 1997).
30 Bob Kauflin, *True Worshipers: Seeking What Matters to God* (Downers Grove, IL: InterVarsity Press, 2005).
31 Kauflin, *True Worshippers*, 121.
32 See James J. S. Harrichand, 'Recovering the Language of Lament for the Western Evangelical Church: A Survey of the Psalms of Lament and Their Appropriation within Pastoral Theology', *McMaster Journal of Theology and Ministry* 16 (2014–2015): 124–25.
33 Kathleen D. Billman and Daniel L. Migliore, *Rachel's Cry: Prayer of Lament and Rebirth of Hope* (Eugene, OR: Wipf and Stock, 1999), vii.
34 Zimmerman, *Worship with Gladness*, 70.

Craig Broyles distinguishes between what he calls 'Psalms of Plea' and 'Psalms of Complaint'. The former, for him, are essentially trusting and praising psalms in which God is asked to intervene on the worshipper's behalf in some way. The latter involve the worshipper questioning why God is either aloof or somehow complicit in the speaker's suffering. However, Broyles affirms that even in the latter, 'The complaints are not complaints per se, but rather intend to summon God to be faithful to his promises and act on the psalmist's behalf.'[35]

The key point, again, is that in the Psalms, the terrible realities of life are taken seriously, allowing a genuine journey of faith and recovery of trust and praise to occur. Papering over the pain does not facilitate faith. Robert S. Smith also highlights the need to challenge any sense of triumphalism in our hymnody: 'Our singing, therefore, needs to reflect the fact that God is not only sovereign over our sufferings but also present with us in them.'[36]

We know how important it is to trust God when our faith is seriously tested. We also know how important hymns and songs are in helping Christians to internalize biblical truths and perspectives. Therefore, we should combine these two affirmations and write hymns and songs that express and reflect the contribution of the psalms of lament to this end.

God wants us to be real in our worship

Zimmerman puts it well:

> God wants us to be ourselves as we come before the divine Majesty to surrender ourselves to God's loving presence. Laments show us that complaining about what is painful for us can lead us to transformation.[37]

The Psalms are firmly based on the realities of life, and that is why they continue to speak to the deepest parts of our lives and cultures. God desires a real relationship with us; the last thing he wants is for us to pretend when we gather to worship him. How many come to church wearing masks, hiding their loneliness, pain, anxiety, guilt, shame or anger?

There are some excellent examples of contemporary Christian songs of lament that also communicate real hope and trust in God. They reflect the survival of some level of demand for authenticity in worship and life, for which we should be glad. I will offer a few examples, from the nineteenth century to the present.

Many of us know the 1873 hymn 'It Is Well with My Soul', which Horatio Spafford wrote amidst unbearable tragedy and grief. In our time, Kristene DiMarco has built on that hymn with 'It Is Well', a song encouraging deep trust for Christians experiencing a crisis of faith. There is no hint of triumphalism or too-easy transition to joy. This is a faith-building song for those who do not feel bright joy. The chorus

---

35 Craig C. Broyles, *The Conflict of Faith and Experience in the Psalms: A Form-Critical and Theological Study* (Sheffield, UK: Sheffield University Press, 1989); see also Collins, *Introduction*, 271–74.
36 Robert S. Smith, 'Belting Out the Blues as Believers: The Importance of Singing Lament', *Themelios* 42, no. 1 (2017): 111.
37 Zimmerman, *Worship with Gladness*, 73.

includes a magnificent piece of poetic writing, drawing in a reference to Jesus calming the storm on the Sea of Galilee:

> So let go, my soul, and trust in him;
> The waves and wind still know his name.[38]

Another example is the song 'How Can I Keep from Singing?' with words from around 1868, but attributed in this commonly found version to Robert Lowry. There have been many versions of this song, but there is a profoundly empathetic quality in the arrangement by Audrey Assad. In the video version, note the understated tone of the music and the choice of a bleak landscape, filmed in black and white, devoid of colour. Typical of the content is the following verse:

> Through all the tumult and the strife,
> I hear the music ringing.
> It finds an echo in my soul.
> How can I keep from singing?[39]

The song encourages us to listen for the echo and to respond to it, however weakly.

Joel Payne's song 'Oh Sisters and Brothers' enables us to stand and sing with those who are far from able to stand by themselves in the face of grief. The chorus, with words of hope and comfort, is nonetheless sung with a melody and arrangement that lack any pressure to sound overtly victorious: 'Though weeping may come in the night, there'll be joy in the morning.'[40]

An example of a song that openly expresses doubts about whether God is really taking care of us as we had hoped and expected—doubts that can buffet all Christians—is 'You Say (Way in the Wilderness)' by Sam Hargreaves. Each verse opens with a challenge to God contained in the words, 'You say …'. Such a song allows us to speak from the heart when many would tell us that doing so is impertinent and will displease God. But we can identify with Job in this song. The final verse confesses:

> You say a new thing is rising up,
> You're bringing new life.
> Right here, this moment, it's feeling tough,
> I'm longing for light.

The final chorus ends with the words, 'You are my way in the wilderness, my faithful God.'[41]

Finally, Andrew Peterson has composed a much bleaker song, writing for those who may experience severe depression in their Christian lives. Doubt, anxiety and fear are present in many of his songs, and they would not be appropriate for every occasion, but when they speak to you, you can hear God calling you close.

---

38 Kristene DiMarco, 'It Is Well', video at https://worldea.org/yourls/ert452riggans2.
39 Audrey Assad, 'How Can I Keep from Singing?' video at https://worldea.org/yourls/ert452riggans3.
40 Joel Payne, 'Oh Sisters and Brothers', video at https://worldea.org/yourls/ert452riggans4.
41 Sam Hargreaves, 'You Say (Way in the Wilderness)', video at https://worldea.org/yourls/ert452riggans5.

One of his songs, 'The Silence of God', has a particularly stark verse. Peterson courageously describes the extra dimension of guilt and despair that can come when sisters or brothers who are in deep distress find themselves surrounded in church by those who cannot mourn with them because they are fixed on the happy ending of our faith. This is perhaps the worst loneliness of all, and Peterson's depiction of the situation is raw:

> And if a man has got to listen to the voices of the mob
> Who are reeling in the throes of all the happiness they've got
> When they tell you all their troubles have been nailed up to that cross
> Then what about the times when even followers get lost?
> 'Cause we all get lost sometimes.[42]

Some of these contemporary songs would be difficult for many congregations to sing corporately. Their contribution to a worship or outreach service might be best facilitated by projecting a video version of the song for people to listen to quietly, letting the words and music speak to them as if this were a testimony being given in church.

To weave Paul's directive to 'mourn with those who mourn' more fully into the fabric of our church hymnodies, we need songs for general congregational worship. Can we not commission songs that will help us move—in real time, as it were—from lament, in fellowship with brothers and sisters, to a recovery of trust in God and a rediscovery of his love for us, and on to a testimony of renewed faith? We can do so if we make proper use of the Psalms, which are God's permission to be real.

---

42 Andrew Peterson, 'The Silence of God', video at https://worldea.org/yourls/ert452riggans6.

Holistic Mission in Biblical and Theological Perspective

Hannes Wiher

For the last 50 years, one of the most important discussions in global evangelicalism has concerned the idea of holistic mission, which proposes the integration of verbal evangelism and social engagement within Christian mission. This article, excerpted from a longer study to be published in the WEA World of Theology Series, examines how key terms such as 'evangelism' and 'mission' are understood in the Bible and in contemporary missiological debates. The author argues for a nuanced holism that recognizes the Bible's overarching concern for our eternal destiny and its endorsement of a wide range of verbal and non-verbal ways to express that concern.

Evangelism and mission in the Bible

In contemporary missiological debates, various participants have defined the key terms 'evangelism' and 'mission' differently, depending on their worldview. The discrepancy recalls the comment by Humpty Dumpty in Lewis Carroll's *Through the Looking-Glass*: 'When I use a word, ... it means just what I choose it to mean, neither more nor less.'[1] But as David Hesselgrave warns, 'A flawed hermeneutic and sub-orthodox view of Scripture allows for a definitional free-for-all in which terms can be redefined without regard for the clear intention of the biblical authors, in which case the world, not the kingdom, sets the agenda.'[2]

For example, 'mission' has been variously described as building the kingdom of God, establishing *shalom*, humanization, participation in the *missio Dei* (God's mission), or everything the church does. But as Anglican bishop Stephen Neill commented, 'If everything is mission, nothing is mission.'[3] John Stott, speaking at the first Lausanne Congress in 1974, also evoked Lewis Carroll to describe the situation: 'The modern church sometimes seems like a kind of theological wonderland in which numerous Humpty Dumptys enjoy playing with words and

---

Hannes Wiher (PhD, Potchefstroom University, South Africa) is president of REMEEF, a network of evangelical missiologists in French-speaking Europe, and co-founder of the journal *Missiologie évangélique* (www.missiologie.net). He has been a professor of missiology at theological seminaries in Asia, Francophone Africa and Europe.

---

1 Lewis Carroll, *Through the Looking-Glass* (Raleigh, NC: Hayes Barton Press, 1872), 72. *Through the Looking-Glass* was Carroll's sequel to *Alice in Wonderland* (1865).
2 David J. Hesselgrave, *Paradigms in Conflict: 10 Key Questions in Christian Missions Today* (Grand Rapids: Kregel, 2005), 346.
3 Stephen C. Neill, *Creative Tension* (London: Edinburgh House, 1959), 81.

making them mean what they want them to mean. ... I shall try to define [the meaning of the words] according to Scripture.'[4]

In an effort to resolve the confusion, I present here a biblical study of key words and concepts related to our being sent on mission and the communication of the gospel. I begin with those terms that one can classify in dichotomizing categories and then discuss those that imply a holistic view of mission. After that, I apply this biblical analysis to current perspectives, including various notions of mission and salvation that are expressed in contemporary missiology.

Biblical terms in the semantic domains of sending and communication

In the Bible, the notion of 'mission' occurs in the form of the verb 'to send' (Hebrew *shalah*, Greek *apostellō* and *pempō*). The concept of sending is very common in both testaments: God sends the patriarchs and the prophets (Gen 6:18; 12:1; Ex 3:10; Isa 6:9; Jer 2:2; Ezek 3:1; Jon 1:2), and 'when the times were fulfilled, God has sent his Son' (Gal 4:4; Jn 3:16). The Son sends his disciples (Mt 10:5; Lk 9:2; 10:1), just as he has been sent (Jn 17:18; 20:21). The sending of the disciples *par excellence* takes place before Jesus' ascension and is confirmed in the final texts of the Gospels and in the beginning of the book of Acts, in what we call the Great Commission (Mt 28:18-20; Mk 16:15-18; Lk 24:44-49; Jn 20:21; Acts 1:8). The sending always implies the functions of witness (Isa 43:10, 12; Rev 1:5; 11:3, 7) and ambassador (2 Cor 5:20). This fact clarifies the relationship between 'mission' (sending) and 'evangelism': generally speaking, Jesus was sent to 'evangelize' (*euangelizomai*), to be a witness (*martys*), to call, gather, form and send his disciples (*mathēteuō*) and to serve (*diakoneō*). God's sending implies that each task is under his Kingdom rule; he specifies the task by his call.

The expression 'preach the Gospel' (or 'proclaim the Gospel,' Greek *keryssō to euangelion*, e.g. Mk 1:38; 16:15), is used on one hand to denote a verbal activity and on the other hand for the total ministry of Jesus and the apostles.[5] For example, *keryssō* is used in the Septuagint of Isaiah 61:1 in parallel to *euangelizomai*. Goldsworthy concludes, 'This eschatological proclamation is the means to obtain liberation and liberty. This proclamation is an integral part of the ministry of Jesus (Mk 1:38; Lk 4:18-19, quoting Isa 61:1-2 and Lk 4:43-44, which links *euangelizomai* and *keryssein*).'[6]

In the missionary mandate of the gospel of Matthew, Jesus commands his disciples to teach (*didaskō*) the nations 'to obey everything that I have commanded you' (Mt 28:20). Jesus not only preaches but teaches everywhere he goes (Lk 23:5). He is known as a teacher (Jn 3:2, 10). The same qualifications of preacher and teacher are attributed to the apostle Paul (Acts 21:28; 2 Tim 1:11). It seems evident that

---

4   John Stott, 'Biblical Basis of Evangelism', in *Let the Earth Hear His Voice: International Congress on World Evangelization, Lausanne, Switzerland*, ed. James D. Douglas (Minneapolis: World Wide Publications, 1975), 65f.
5   See the occurrences of *keryssō to euangelion* in the sense of verbal proclamation of the gospel: Mt 4:23 (preach the gospel and heal); 1 Thess 2:2 (say the gospel), and in the sense of the total ministry of Jesus and the apostles, Mt 24:14 and parallels; Mt 26:13; Mk 1:14; 13:10; 16:15; Acts 20:24 (witness the gospel); Rom 1:1 ('evangelize the gospel').
6   Graeme L. Goldsworthy, 'Gospel', *New Dictionary of Biblical Theology*, ed. B. Rosner and T. Alexander (Leicester, UK: IVP, 2000), 577.

teaching is a process of verbal communication. However, does teaching limit itself to words? Does the fact that Jesus gathers the disciples around him before sending them (Mk 3:13–15) not imply a more encompassing pedagogical process?

The biblical use of the verb 'evangelize' also allows for two interpretations, both of which we find among evangelical theologians. On one hand, *euangelizomai* can denote verbal proclamation of the gospel.[7] From this point of view, evangelism has priority over social action because it deals with the eternal destiny of man. Advocates of this approach distinguish evangelism from mission, which in this view usually includes all verbal and non-verbal activities related to the proclamation and the presentation of the gospel. On the other hand, *euangelizomai* can denote all the activities of Jesus' and the apostles' ministry, including all aspects of the communication of the gospel, not limited to verbal proclamation.[8] In this interpretation, evangelism is synonymous with the notions of 'making disciples' and 'mission'. From this point of view, the eternal destiny of man has the priority independently of whether a verbal or a non-verbal activity is involved. The first interpretation is the traditional evangelical position and that of the Lausanne Movement before the turn of the millennium; the second is that of the Cape Town Commitment and the Micah Network. The second interpretation encompasses the first and leads to the notion of integral or holistic mission.

We continue with two terms that denote an action: 'heal' (*therapeuō*) and 'cast out demons' (*ekballō ta daimonia*). They can denote the simple act of healing and casting out demons (Mt 8:13, 16; 12:15, 22; 14:14; 15:30; 19:2; 21:14 and parallels; Mk 1:34; 16:17f; Luke 14:4; Acts 3:6; 10:38). They are often used in opposition to a term denoting a verbal activity. For example, it is said of God that 'he sent out his word and healed [*rafa'*] them' (Ps 107:20). Jesus preaches the gospel of the kingdom, casts out demons and heals (Mt 4:23f; 9:32f). And he sends his disciples to preach, heal and cast out demons (Mt 10:7f; Mk 3:14f; 16:15, 17).

The situation is a little more complex for the term 'serve' (*diakoneō*), which in English clearly denotes a social, non-verbal activity. In allusion to the 'Servant of the Lord' (*'ebed yhwh*) of Isaiah 42–53, service carries a more general sense. In this vein,

---

7 For the verbal proclamation of the gospel, see the following occurrences of *euangelizomai*: Lk 4:43 (parallel to preach in v. 44); Lk 9:6 (evangelize and heal); Lk 20:1 and Acts 5:42 (teach and evangelize); Acts 8:4 and 15:35 ('evangelize' the word); Acts 8:25 (witness, say and evangelize); Acts 8:35 (open the mouth and evangelize); Acts 10:36 (announce peace); Acts 11:20 (say and evangelize); Acts 13:32 (announce the gospel of promise); Acts 17:18 (parallel with babbler); Rom 1:15; 10:15 (parallel between preaching, sending and evangelization); 1 Cor 1:17 (parallel with the word); 1 Cor 15:1 (the gospel that I have taught); Heb 4:2, 6 and 1 Peter 1:25 (parallel with the word).

8 For the total ministry of Jesus and the apostles, see the following occurrences of *euangelizomai*: Mt 11:5 and Lk 4:18–19 (if one considers the sequence of mentioned actions as a synonymic parallelism); Lk 16:16; Acts 14:7; 16:10; Rom 10:15 (parallel between preaching, sending and evangelization); Rom 15:20; 1 Cor 9:16, 18; 2 Cor 10:16; 11:7; Gal 1:8, 11, 16, 23; 4:13; Eph 2:17; 3:8; 1 Thess 3:6; 1 Pet 1:12. For an argument in favour of an interpretation of the notion of 'proclamation of the gospel' in the sense of the total ministry of Jesus and the apostles, see John Stott, *Christian Mission in the Modern World* (London: Falcon, 1975; rpt. Downers Grove, IL: InterVarsity Press, 2013), 25–87; Ulrich Becker, 'Gospel, Evangelize, Evangelist', *New International Dictionary of the New Testament*, vol. 2, ed. Colin Brown, rev. ed. (Carlisle, UK: Paternoster; Grand Rapids, MI: Zondervan, 1986), 111, 113. Becker supports this interpretation particularly in relation to Paul's usage of *euangelizomai*.

Jesus says, 'I am among you as one who serves' (Lk 22:27), and 'Just as the Son of Man came not to be served but to serve, and to give his life a ransom for many' (Mt 20:28). Service is here linked with the propitiatory sacrifice of the Servant of the Lord. Later on, the notion extends to the general ministry of the apostles, such as Paul: 'I am on my way to Jerusalem in the service of the Lord's people there' (Rom 15:25). For him and his collaborators, the term can denote the overall ministry (*diakonia*, 2 Cor 8:19; 1 Tim 3:10, 13; 1 Pet 1:12; 4:10).

The task given to Jesus' disciples, or their service (ministry), is 'to make disciples' (*mathēteuō*, Mt 28:19). This is according to Jesus' example of calling the disciples around him in order to send them (Mk 3:13-15). Their process of sharing life together during a period of several years implies a process of transformation with many verbal and non-verbal pedagogical components. As the Father has sent the Son, Jesus sends his disciples (Jn 17:18; 20:21) to repeat this pedagogical process with others (Mt 28:19). To make disciples is apparently an integral ministry.

The verb 'to witness' (*martyreō*) and notions of 'being a witness' (*eimi martys*) or of witness itself (*martyria*) are equally a matter of the total person. The people of Israel had been called to be the witness ('*ed*) for God, his uniqueness and his liberating acts (Isa 43:10, 12; 44:8). The Servant of the Lord is the Witness par excellence (Isa 43:10; 55:4). Following him, Jesus is the Witness to the truth (John 18:37), the 'faithful Witness' (Rev 1:5). Witness is also at the centre of the two Lukan missionary mandates:

> And he said to them, 'Thus it is written, that the Messiah is to suffer and to rise from the dead on the third day, and that repentance and forgiveness of sins are to be proclaimed in his name to all nations, beginning from Jerusalem. You are witnesses of these things.' (Lk 24:46-48)

> But you will receive power when the Holy Spirit has come upon you; and you will be my witnesses in Jerusalem, in all Judea and Samaria, and to the ends of the earth. (Acts 1:8)

Peter and Paul, and the apostles in general, are witnesses for Jesus, his life and his acts (Acts 2:32; 3:15; 5:32; 10:39; 22:15; 23:11; 1 Pet 5:1; Rev 11:3, 7; 17:6). It is astonishing that the notion of witness did not carry greater importance in missiology before the second half of the twentieth century. Concerning the witness of the Church, Lesslie Newbigin introduces the concept of an 'ecclesiological hermeneutic' to underscore its importance and holistic character:

> The whole life of the church, understood correctly, is the visible means by which the Holy Spirit accomplishes His mission in the world, and thus the totality of the life of the church participates in her character of witness. The whole life of the church has thus a missionary dimension, even if it does not have mission as primary intention.[9]

Although the concept of 'mission' includes several terms with either a dichotomizing or holistic connotation, the Bible also uses metaphors to speak of the

---

9   Lesslie Newbigin, *One Body, One Gospel, One World: The Christian Mission Today* (London and New York: International Missionary Council, 1958), 21.

communication of the good news, usually in a holistic manner. I will mention four examples here.

First, the law prescribes *salt* as a means to conserve and flavour food to be part of the offerings. In this way, salt has become a symbol of the faithfulness and steadfastness of the covenants in the Ancient Near East in general and of God's covenant with Israel in particular. In this perspective, the Old Testament speaks of the 'salt of your God's covenant' (Lev 2:13; cf. Num 18:19; 2 Chron 13:5). Jesus is referring to this cultural background when he says of his disciples, 'You are the salt of the earth; but if salt has lost its taste, how can its saltiness be restored?' (Mt 5:13).

Second, since ancient times, *light* has represented the presence and the favour of God (cf. Ps 27:2; Isa 9:2; 2 Cor 4:6). In the present context, it symbolizes the radiance of the good news. In this sense, the Servant of the Lord is called to be a light for the nations (Isa 42:6). Jesus, the Servant of the Lord par excellence, is himself the Light (Jn 1:4–9), and he charges the disciples to be the 'light of the world' (Mt 5:14–16).

The Bible mentions two other metaphors that indicate the radiance of the good news. 'You show that you are a *letter* of Christ ... written ... with the Spirit of the living God' (2 Cor 3:3). The Christians are also compared to a *fragrance* for their environment: 'For we are to God the pleasing aroma of Christ among those who are being saved and those who are perishing. To the one we are an aroma that brings death; to the other, an aroma that brings life' (2 Cor 2:15f, NIV). Evidently, according to the Bible, these metaphors evoke Christian witness as a whole, verbal and non-verbal.

Missiological concepts in the light of the Bible

We have seen that the Bible presents sending ('mission') as an underlying element of all tasks involved in the communication of the good news. In this way, it distinguishes itself in a significant way from the usage of the term in the missiological debate of the Lausanne Movement, as a concept encompassing several modes of communication. On the other hand, the Bible presents evangelism as a term that can denote the verbal proclamation of the gospel, in continuity with the usage in the Lausanne Movement, but also, in contrast, as a term denoting the whole ministry of Jesus and the apostles. Other biblical terms for mission can also denote the totality of communication, both verbal and non-verbal.

Concerning the two concepts of evangelism and social action, according to Timothy Tennent, professor of missiology and president of Asbury Theological Seminary (USA), the Old Testament identifies three qualities of God's character:[10] justice (*mishpat*), loving kindness (*hesed*) and compassion (*rahamim*). God demonstrates them through his particular concern for four groups of persons: widows, orphans, immigrants and the poor (Ex 22:21f; Ps 68:5; 82:3f; Isa 10:2; Jer 22:3). God's people have to reflect God's character. The evaluation of these three attitudes is found in people's behaviour towards the marginalized on a personal level (Ex 22:27; Lev 19:9f; 23:22; Deut 24:19–21) and on a structural level (Ex 12:49; 23:2; Lev 24:22; Prov 29:14; Isa 10:1; Jer 22:16; Mal 3:5).

---

10 In this discussion, I follow Timothy C. Tennent, 'Reflecting the Incarnation in Holistic Missions', in *Invitation to World Missions: A Trinitarian Missiology for the Twenty-first Century* (Grand Rapids: Zondervan, 2010), 387–406.

In the New Testament, Jesus is born into a poor family (Jn 1:46) and identifies himself with the poor and the marginalized. Luke/Acts demonstrates this fact especially strongly. In the Magnificat, Mary situates herself among the poor (Lk 1:52f). Jesus announces the Good News to the poor (Lk 4:18) and declares the poor blessed and honourable (Mt 5:3; Lk 6:20). This blessing places in tension the persons who are spiritually poor, i.e. those who consider themselves in need of God and his forgiveness (Mt 5:3), and those who are globally and materially poor (Lk 6:20). For Jesus, even the rich, and maybe especially them, can be spiritually blind or poor (Lk 12:16–21; 16:19–31). This identification with the poor, crippled, paralysed and blind is put in an eschatological context in the parable of the great banquet (Lk 14:13f; Mt 22:9f) and the parable of the sheep and the goats (Mt 25:31-46). Interestingly, in these passages, Jesus will receive those who will have been involved in social action! Beyond the identification with the poor, Jesus heals the sick as a sign of the kingdom of God to come (Lk 7:22; 11:20) and sends the disciples to do the same (Mt 10:7f; Lk 9:1–6; 10:1–16). This eschatological perspective continues in the book of Acts in the ministry of the apostles: the paralysed walk (Acts 3:1–10; 14:8–10), the blind see (Acts 9:1–18), the doors of prisons open (Acts 5:19; 16:26). Here we see a predominance of non-verbal communication.

On the other hand, in many cases Jesus begins his proclamation of the good news of the kingdom with a call to repentance, starting with Mark 1:14f. The apostles continue this method of proclamation in the book of Acts, starting with Peter at Pentecost (Acts 2:38) and continuing with Paul who stated, 'We preach Christ crucified' (1 Cor 1:23). These are instances of predominantly verbal communication of the gospel.

To sum up these observations, Tennent speaks of a 'paradigm of evangelism' and a 'paradigm of social action'. However, he notes, 'Once evangelism and social action are conceptualized as two separate spheres, it is inevitable that evangelism is given a priority over social action.'[11] A theologian with a dichotomizing worldview will tend to see separate concepts, make distinctions and define priorities. In contrast, a theologian with a holistic worldview will see the whole and may not understand the relevance of distinctions. We can see this tension in the various ways in which people understand evangelism and mission. The notion of holistic or integral mission can finally lead to not making distinctions at all, as for example Bryant Myers or Ronald Sider seem to propose.[12] On the other hand, despite their holistic perspective, the Micah Declaration still distinguishes between evangelism and transformation, and the Cape Town Commitment distinguishes witness of truth from witness of life.

Tennent argues, from a holistic perspective, in favour of recognizing 'the fundamental unity between word and deed'.[13] He also urges that we 'resist individualism that does not make room for various gifts and graces in the body of Christ.'[14] From his holistic perspective, Tennent provides this definition of evangelism:

---

11 Tennent, 'Reflecting', 393.
12 Bryant Myers, 'Holistic Mission: New Frontiers', in *Holistic Mission. God's Plan for God's People*, eds. Brian Woolnough and Wonsuk Ma (Oxford: Regnum, 2010), 119–27; Ronald J. Sider, 'Words and Deeds', *Journal of Theology for Southern Africa* 29 (December 1979): 47.
13 Tennent, 'Reflecting', 399.
14 Tennent, 'Reflecting', 403.

> [Evangelism] is not merely about discipling *individuals*; it is about our summoning the *entire culture* to the inbreaking realities of the New Creation. Evangelism is the permeation of the whole gospel into every aspect of a culture and demonstrating, through word and deed, what it means to be 'in Christ'. Evangelism is not just about our 'doing'; it is fundamentally about our 'being'. The church is to be a community of health, demonstrating through our words and actions the qualities of justice (*mishpat*), kindness/faithfulness (*hesed*), and compassion (*rahamim*).[15]

For John Stott, here also writing from a holistic perspective, there are three reasons for the integration of the different dimensions of Christian witness.[16] The first deals with the character of God, who is both Creator and Redeemer. He is interested in the total well-being of man created in his image and wants him to live in abundance. In return, he demands a total allegiance from his people. Micah 6:8, the watchword of the Micah Network, expresses these imperatives well: 'He has told you, O mortal, what is good; and what does the Lord require of you but to do justice [*mishpat*], and to love kindness [*hesed*], and to walk humbly with your God?' The first recommendation in this verse concerns the reciprocal relationship between human beings, the second indicates a proper attitude towards the needy, and the third involves our attitude towards our Creator. Understood in this way, Micah 6:8 encompasses all the situations of human life. The Law and the Prophets reveal God's character, and we should witness to him in the same holistic way.

The second reason for integration, according to Stott, deals with Jesus' ministry and teaching: 'Jesus' words explained his actions, and the former eloquently demonstrated the latter. ... Words without acts lack credibility; acts without words lack clarity. Jesus' actions rendered his words visible; his words rendered his acts intelligible.'[17]

The third reason for integration, according to Stott, relates to the communication of the gospel. Communication studies remind us that the most effective communication includes both verbal and non-verbal components.[18] Followers of Jesus should not neglect verbal witness, but we should also render our words visible in our lives, just as God rendered his Word visible in Jesus Christ (Jn 1:14). Just as God shares our concerns, our suffering and our struggles in Jesus, he calls us to enter into the social reality of our neighbours. Through this integration, our acts 'become preaching', as Johan Bavinck says.[19]

---

15 Tennent, 'Reflecting', 404–5; emphasis in the original.
16 John Stott, 'Holistic Mission,' in Stott, *The Contemporary Christian: Applying God's Word to Today's World* (Downers Grove, IL: IVP, 1992), 343–49.
17 Stott, 'Holistic Mission', 346.
18 Paul Watzlawick, Janet H. Helminck-Beavin and Don D. Jackson, *Pragmatics of Human Communication: A Study of Interactional Patterns, Pathologies, and Paradoxes* (New York: W. W. Norton & Co., 1967).
19 Johan H. Bavinck, *An Introduction to the Science of Missions* (Philadelphia: Presbyterian and Reformed, 1960), 113, quoted by Stott, 'Holistic Mission', 349.

Conceptions of mission and salvation

Our worldview influences not only our theological and missiological positions, but also our biblical interpretations. This dynamic can be observed in the debate over where mission starts in the Bible. Several options have been proposed. I will start with the most traditional view and work backwards.

Does mission start with Jesus Christ's propitiatory death on the cross and his resurrection? The Protestant missionary movement of the nineteenth century adopted this approach, according to which the Great Commission of Matthew 28 carries supreme importance for mission. An important representative of this position, David Bosch, devoted just four of 500 pages in his 1991 book *Transforming Mission* to mission in the Old Testament. This option implies a relatively narrow definition of mission and salvation.

Does mission start with the ministry of Jesus? Luke 4:18f. has frequently been cited in this way within the ecumenical movement, by radical evangelicals and by the Micah Network. In Luke 4, the definition of mission and salvation is broad, including not only eternal salvation but also physical, social and political aspects. However, these groups tend not to highlight the effusion of the Holy Spirit (v. 22) and the forgiveness of sins (v. 23). The parallel passage of John 20:21 is also quoted often by these circles and was emphasized by John Stott. Missiology has tended to neglect these two passages in the past.

Does mission start with Abraham's sending in Genesis 12? Abraham is blessed and mandated to be a blessing for all the families of the earth. The New Testament often refers to Abraham. The notion of blessing as stated in the Cape Town Commitment could encompass this creational and missionary mandate. However, certain interpreters introduce a dichotomy between material and spiritual dimensions into the notion of blessing.

Does mission start with the Fall in Genesis 3? In this case, the objective would be the restoration of the relationship between God and mankind. It would be logical for a solution to be offered immediately after the problem has emerged. The representatives of this option tend to distinguish clearly between the creational and the missionary mandate. This implies narrow definitions of mission and salvation, limited to the eternal destiny of man.

Does mission start with the declaration of biblical monotheism in Genesis 1? A distinction between the creational and missionary mandate would become meaningless, or at least difficult to sustain, in this option. On the other hand, the notions of mission and salvation would become quite broad. This is the position of Christopher Wright, coordinator of the Theological Commission of the Lausanne Movement, in his 2006 book *The Mission of God*.

As for why someone may prefer one of these options, it seems that one's foundational worldview, which is mostly subconscious, may play a role. Each approach tends to base its theology of mission on one or two key verses. They do not develop a theology of mission that draws on the missional dimension of the whole Bible, i.e. a missional hermeneutic of the Bible as Christopher Wright recommends.[20]

---

20 Christopher J. H. Wright, 'Searching for a Missional Hermeneutic', in Wright, *The Mission of God: Unlocking God's Narrative* (Downers Grove, IL: InterVarsity Press, 2006), 33–47.

Assessment of the biblical analysis

The preceding review of relevant words and concepts in the Bible has shown that the same terms can denote verbal or non-verbal activity, or sometimes both. This is particularly the case for such activities as 'preach the Gospel', 'evangelize', 'teach' and 'serve'. It may be surprising to some that certain terms, which we generally classify as referring to the verbal proclamation of the gospel, sometimes also denote the whole ministry of Jesus and the apostles.

The use of certain terms in the missiological debates of the Lausanne Movement has differed somewhat from the semantic domain found in the Bible. This is for example the case for the Bible's use of 'preach the gospel' or 'evangelize' in a holistic as well as a verbal perspective, whereas the Lausanne Movement used them in an exclusively verbal sense before the turn of the millennium. In the Cape Town Commitment, its non-verbal aspects are rendered by the expression 'witness of life'. This observation is also valid for the notion of 'sending' (mission), which has acquired a completely new meaning in the contemporary theological and missiological discourse, covering a variety of communicative activities. For the Bible, on the other hand, sending refers to God's initiating process that underlies the communication of the gospel.

Theologians with a dichotomizing worldview tend towards narrow and well-defined semantic domains, as illustrated by the first declarations of the Lausanne Movement. They introduce distinctions and nuances in their theology and missiology, such as the distinction between evangelism and social responsibility (with priority usually given to evangelism). In contrast, for theologians with a holistic worldview, a separation of different dimensions of Christian witness does not make sense. They tend towards large and fuzzy semantic domains and perceive not divergences but convergences between the terms.

In the Bible, mission consists of a multiple witness: witnessing to the messianic King and his life, death and resurrection, proclaiming the Good News, making disciples of the nations, going into the whole world, baptizing in his name, teaching all that Jesus has commanded, warning of divine judgement, healing the sick, casting out demons, receiving the power of the Holy Spirit, and experiencing the presence of Christ. In other words, the components of proclamation, persuasion, dialogue, prophetic criticism, silent presence and social action are all present in mission.

A Nuanced Holism

I will now analyse the contributions of the notion of holistic or integral mission to the missiological debate, along with some shortcomings. I will propose an alternative articulation of holism that, I believe, makes the necessary biblical distinctions.

Positive contributions

The concept of holistic mission combines things that actually belong together. In this way, it moves beyond the dichotomizing concepts of 'multiple witness', introduced by Western theology of mission.[21] The same observation applies to the term 'transformation', which has replaced the expression 'holistic mission' in many instances. It helps to restore a proper biblical balance between orthodoxy and orthopraxy.

Lack of distinctions and nuances

Western theologians, operating generally from a dichotomizing worldview, have criticized the concept of holistic mission because it does not present the necessary distinctions. This criticism is certainly valid for some, but not for the Lausanne Movement, the Micah Network or the radical evangelicals, except perhaps for a few exceptions such as Ronald Sider's comment of 40 years ago, 'The time has come for all Christians to refuse to use the sentence: "The primary task of the Church is" … .'[22]

The Bible presents a holistic worldview, with the important qualification that it conceives of the created universe as opposed to its creator. In this way, the Hebrew worldview places the holistic and dichotomizing worldviews in tension. As David Hesselgrave remarks, the Bible 'begins with an absolute dichotomy between the Creator and his creation. It proceeds by making very different valuations of body and soul, treasures on earth and treasures in heaven, and this world and the world to come.'[23] The Bible makes thus important distinctions within a generally holistic approach. The Grand Rapids Report (1982) perceives these distinctions in a rather negative way but affirms at the same time that the Bible sets them in tension:

> We tend to set over against one another in an unhealthy way soul and body, the individual and society, redemption and creation, grace and nature, heaven and earth, justification and justice, faith and works. The Bible certainly distinguishes between these, but it also relates them to each other, and it instructs us to hold each pair in a dynamic and creative tension.[24]

On the other hand, Hesselgrave sees these distinctions in a positive way and prioritizes them based on an essentially dichotomizing worldview:

> With reference to spiritual transformation and social transformation, it gives priority to spiritual transformation. With reference to spirit, mind, and body, it gives priority to the spirit or soul. With reference to social action and evangelism, it gives priority to evangelism. In maintaining these priorities, however, it does not admit to being reductionistic.[25]

---

21 Examples of multiple witness include the traditional two mandates (creational and evangelistic), the triple mandate (Micah's being, doing and speaking, or the Ecumenical Movement's proclamation, fellowship and service), Evert Van de Poll's fourfold mandate (personal and collective witness, proclamation and service), and the Anglican Communion's five marks of mission (proclaiming the Good News, teaching, baptizing and nurturing believers, responding to human need, transforming unjust structures and safeguarding creation).
22 Sider, 'Words and Deeds', 47.
23 Hesselgrave, *Paradigms in Conflict*, 123.
24 Lausanne Movement, *Evangelism and Social Responsibility: An Evangelical Commitment*, LOP 21: The Grand Rapids Report, 4A, https://worldea.org/yourls/ert452wiher1.
25 Hesselgrave, *Paradigms in Conflict*, 121.

The eternal destiny of man and holistic mission

Another aspect towards which very little reflection has been devoted is the relationship between concern for the eternal destiny of man and for his material and social needs. It can be very difficult to manage proclamation of the gospel and social responsibility harmoniously side by side. Social action always demands a huge amount of time, energy and financial resources and risks marginalizing the preoccupation for people's eternal destiny. In several evangelical individuals and organizations, a 'drift' has been observed towards more and more engagement in humanitarian responsibilities with the result that finally no resources were left for engaging with matters of spiritual salvation.[26]

Rather than speaking about the dichotomy between evangelism and social responsibility that has animated the discussions in the Lausanne Movement, I would propose another duality: on one hand, the Bible places great emphasis on people's eternal destiny; on the other hand, it recognizes great liberty in the choice of communicative strategies, verbal and non-verbal. We can perhaps capture this duality in the expression 'Christocentric *shalom*', which combines a holistic approach with an emphasis on Christ and the salvation he offers.[27]

The mission of Jesus and of the disciples

The promotors of holistic mission see themselves as continuing Jesus' mission. As Jesus, the Word of God, has incarnated himself in the world (Jn 1:14), Jesus' disciples are called to 'incarnate' the values of the reign of Christ in their imitation of Christ. Thus, Jesus' life becomes the model for the disciples' life.

However, there are aspects of discontinuity as well as continuity between the disciples' mission and that of Jesus. Obviously, Jesus was unique in his incarnation and propitiatory death on the cross. The apostle Paul sees himself as an ambassador of the unique Christ event ('we preach Christ crucified', 1 Cor 1:23) and imitator of Christ (1 Cor 11:1; Phil 2:5–11), but much more as his witness. According to Hesselgrave, the Bible defends the discontinuity of the different missions, and continuity only in the relationship between the Lord and his disciple:

> The Son had one mission, the Twelve another, the Seventy or Seventy-two another (Mt 10; Lk 10), and those who respond to the Great Commission of Matthew 28 and Mark 16 yet another. … By maintaining that the church's mission is a continuation of Christ's own personal mission, [one] blurs these distinctions. … Paul maintains continuity in the sender–sendee relationship but progression in the divine program of redemption (2 Cor 5:20).[28]

Eschatology and holistic mission

In the missiological debate, commonly very little is said about the eschatological problem of our position in the epoch between the two comings of Jesus Christ. It

---

26 See Peirong Lin, *Countering Mission Drift in a Faith-based Organization: An Interdisciplinary Theological Interpretation Focused on the Case Study of World Vision's Identity Formation* (Bonn: VKW, 2019), summarized in 'The Case for Practical Theological Interpretation in Faith-based Organizations', *Evangelical Review of Theology* 42, no. 4 (2018): 319–33.
27 I am indebted to Erwan Cloarec for this expression.
28 Hesselgrave, *Paradigms in Conflict*, 152.

was not Jesus' intent to heal all diseases during his life on earth. Evangelicals' energetic support of the United Nations' Sustainable Development Goals could encourage us to adopt this idea. Certainly, we should be engaged in local and global efforts to alleviate suffering. But Jesus came primarily to show the character of the reign of God by his life of compassion and his signs of healing (Mt 11:4f; Lk 11:20) and to die on the cross for the sins of humanity (Mk 10:45 par.). The victory over evil and sin is already accomplished in the spiritual world, but not yet in our material world. Our struggle against sickness, misery and poverty continues.

In this regard, biblical teaching corresponds to an inaugurated but not yet completed eschatology. The marginalization of this teaching can lead to a worldly activism that presumes that we have to create the conditions for the return of Christ (a postmillennialist position). It can also induce an attitude of fatalism, letting world situations degenerate until God's intervention (a premillennialist position). Moreover, the lack of sound knowledge of the Bible can lead to the prosperity gospel or to dominion theology, both of which act as if the ideal state is already attained or within reach (a realized eschatology).

Conclusion

In debates over the semantic domain of mission and the relationship between evangelism and social responsibility, there is an identifiable conflict between theologies of the Global North and South, which is highly relevant in the context of the present transfer of the centre of gravity of global Christianity. In addition, differing worldviews influence theologians' Bible interpretation and the conception of mission, although the Bible itself holds aspects of holistic and dichotomizing worldviews in tension.

One may be tempted to conclude with David Bosch that 'ultimately mission remains undefinable', even in Scripture.[29] For Bosch, the debate between evangelical and ecumenical voices points to the influence of differing worldviews. He assesses the competing views as partial and complementary.[30] The debates on evangelism, social responsibility and mission in the Lausanne Movement indicate an analogous explanation for the differing positions of theologians from the Global North and South. Generally speaking, the former group in each pair leans towards a dichotomizing and the latter towards a holistic worldview. My biblical analysis seems to confirm Bosch's perspective in this regard.

Overall, the biblical record assures us that the different dimensions of Christian witness are all important. Words explain being and actions, and the latter confirm the words. At the same time, the preoccupation of the Bible with the eternal destiny of man, and the liberty of God and of his envoys in their choice of communicative strategies, should orient our understanding of evangelism and mission.

---

29 David Bosch, *Transforming Mission: Paradigm Shifts in Theology of Mission* (Maryknoll, NY: Orbis, 1991), 9.
30 David Bosch, *Witness to the World: The Christian Mission in Theological Perspective* (Atlanta: John Knox Press; London: Marshall, Morgan & Scott, 1980), 202–20.

Reconciling God's Justice and His Sovereignty in the Process of Salvation: Towards a Mediating View Between Causative Faith and Reprobation

Daniel Kirkpatrick

How can we consider God just if he has decided in advance that some people will not be saved? That is one of the foremost problems in apologetics. This article reviews the range of answers given in church history and proposes a solution.

Introduction

Why are some sinners condemned to eternal demise while others experience eternal glories? This question became prominent at the time of Augustine of Hippo, but it is present in Scripture itself, notably in Romans 9.[1] Of particular concern is whether the *cause* of eternal retribution is intrinsic or extrinsic to the sinner; that is, are sinners condemned because of their own sins, or because of God's immutable decree? In this article, I begin with an historical survey of the issue. Along with describing the views of those who emphasize God's right to decree as he wishes, I also examine those who have advocated for *conditional* election as a way to exonerate God from moral evil for allegedly giving people no chance to avoid condemnation. I will then try to develop a tenable response to the charges lodged against God's justice, affirming unconditional election without resorting to reprobation by immutable decree.

Most of the Western church during the fifth century sided with Augustine with regard to predestination. Augustine contended, contrary to Pelagius, that humans cannot gain salvation through any residual goodness found within themselves, as though they had the power to cooperate with God to attain salvation.[2] By divine

---

Daniel Kirkpatrick (PhD, University of Wales) is Associate Professor of Christian Studies and Dean of the College of Arts and *Sciences* at University of the Southwest, Hobbs, NM, USA. He is the author of Monergism or Synergism? (Pickwick, 2018) and numerous journal articles.

---

1 Matthew Levering, 'Roman Catholic View', in *Five Views on the Extent of the Atonement*, ed. Adam J. Johnson (Grand Rapids: Zondervan, 2019), 88–89.
2 Lenka Karfíková, *Grace and the Will According to Augustine* (Leiden: Brill, 2012), 167–81.

decree, the elect were appointed to salvation apart from foreseen faith.[3] Salvation is based on God's grace and no one can be saved in any other way. Naturally, this leads one to question the fate of those not appointed to salvation. Were they appointed to damnation by just as firm a divine decree?

I cannot fully explore the famous fifth-century Pelagian controversy here, but the literature in that debate focused largely on the question of human freedom and ability. Pelagius believed that Adam's sin was not transmitted to the whole human race but was limited to the historic Adam himself (thus leaving the rest of us with the freedom, or *possibilitas*, to live the life God requires).[4]

However, the Pelagian controversy also entailed considerations of God's moral goodness and justice that are often overlooked. Pelagius declared, 'It is unjust that the soul which is only recently produced, and that not out of Adam's substance, should bear the sin of another committed so long ago.'[5] God would (according to Pelagius) be implicated with evil should he condemn people for actions that were not their own while also requiring humans to do what they were incapable of doing.[6] What is at stake in this debate, therefore, goes beyond the integrity of the human will to the integrity of the divine nature.

Likewise, God's justice and goodness were also a central concern for Julian of Eclanum, a formidable advocate of Pelagianism. 'We maintain', Julian said, 'that men are the work of God, and that no one is forced unwillingly by His [God's] power either into evil or good, but that man does either good or ill of his own will.'[7] To attribute the behaviour of unwilling persons to extrinsic factors would make the author of that external force culpable of an immoral act. God, according to Julian, does not operate in such a way.

Augustine (and the subsequent Councils of Carthage and Orange) would defend the justice of God against these concerns. In doing so, they followed an historic pattern in explaining the cause(s) of condemnation. However, others have not been persuaded by their defence, maintaining that to give anything other than intrinsic causes for condemnation is to attribute injustice (and thus evil) to God. For example, many centuries later Jacobus Arminius held that such an explanation would make God the efficient and sufficient cause of sinners' condemnation rather than the sinners themselves—thus implying that God would be morally responsible for evil, which cannot be.[8] Arminius and others rejected the idea that sinners perished simply because they were not elect, rather than because of their sins. From this stance, it

---

3 Augustine, 'On Rebuke and Grace', in *Nicene and Post-Nicene Fathers*, ed. Philip Schaff, vol. 5 (Peabody, MA: Hendrickson, 2012), 489 (chapter 42).
4 Anton Adamut, 'Some Aspects of the Pelagian Controversy', *Hermeneia* 16 (2016): 129–31.
5 Pelagius as quoted in Augustine, 'On Forgiveness of Sins, and Baptism', in Schaff, *Nicene and Post-Nicene Fathers*, 5:76.
6 Jonathan Hill, *The History of Christian Thought* (Downers Grove, IL: InterVarsity Press, 2003), 78.
7 Julian as quoted by Augustine, 'Against Two Letters of the Pelagians', in Schaff, *Nicene and Post-Nicene Fathers*, 5:388.
8 Jacobus Arminius, 'On Predestination to Salvation, and On Damnation Considered in the Highest Degree', in *The Works of James Arminius*, vol. 2 (Spring Valley, CA: Lamp Post, 2009), 332–33. See also Arminius, 'On Predestination' in *The Works of James Arminius*, 1:166.

followed logically that if the cause for condemnation must reside within the individual, then salvation too must be dependent on the will of the individual.

Robust responses to the charges against God's justice are evident throughout church history. Augustine (who affirmed reprobation by immutable decree) believed sinners were justly condemned for their wilful sin to which they were enslaved, thus absolving God of guilt.[9] Throughout the Protestant Reformation, John Calvin also defended the justice of God, affirming that God incurs no guilt by condemning the wicked according to an immutable decree.[10] Article 1 of the 1618–1619 Canons of Dort, which rejected Arminius' views, begins with a defence of God's justice concerning reprobation. However, critics have not been convinced.

Defining reprobation

Before I assess the arguments as to whether reprobation by divine decree can be associated with moral evil, I must first define the term 'reprobation'. The Greek noun often translated as 'reprobation' is *adokimos*, and its use is fairly rare.[11] It is commonly translated as 'unqualified, worthless, base'; its antonym, *dokimos*, refers to 'testing' or 'certifying' something to be true.[12] Particularly in Paul's usage, *adokimos* refers to those whose faith was disingenuous and would not withstand the test of time (or of eschatological judgement).[13]

Theologically, reprobation has been understood primarily in two different ways: passive or active. The passive view (often called *preterition*) refers to God predestining the non-elect to remain in their state of wilful rebellion and abandoning them in that estate, leading to their just condemnation.[14] Wayne Grudem (in a way similar to the Canons of Dort) defines reprobation as 'the sovereign decision of God before creation to pass over some persons, in sorrow deciding not to save them, and to punish them for their sins, and thereby to manifest his justice'.[15] Notice the words 'in sorrow', which nuance the definition to suggest that God chose in eternity past to pass over some persons, albeit with a degree of regret. Two noteworthy takeaways from this view are that God is still the reason why persons are in hell and that such reprobation is done passively.

The more active way of defining reprobation is often called *double predestination*. This view claims that God assigns persons to dishonour, wrath and eternal demise as a way to demonstrate his justice.[16] Calvin was one notable

---

9 Augustine, 'On Rebuke and Grace', 489. See also Augustine, 'On the Gift of Perseverance', chap. 16.
10 John Calvin, *Institutes of the Christian Religion*, 3.21.5, 7; 3.23.3; 3.24.14.
11 The word appears in Rom 1:28; 1 Cor 9:27; 2 Cor 13:5–7; 2 Tim 3:8; Tit 1:16; Heb 6:8.
12 Walter Bauer, *A Greek-English Lexicon of the New Testament*, ed. and trans. William F. Arndt, F. Wilber Gingrich and Frederick W. Danker, 3rd ed. (Chicago: University of Chicago Press, 2000), s.v. *adokimos, dokimos*.
13 Gerhard Kittel, ed., *Theological Dictionary of the New Testament*, vol. 2 (Grand Rapids: Eerdmans, 1978), s.v. *dokimos*.
14 This view was articulated by Augustine in 'On Rebuke and Grace', chap. 42. It is also held by those who adhere to the Canons of Dort and the Westminster Standards.
15 Wayne Grudem, *Systematic Theology* (Grand Rapids: Zondervan, 1994), 685.
16 See Louis Berkhof, *Systematic Theology* (Grand Rapids: Eerdmans, 1976), 116; Daniel

proponent of this position. Although Calvin's views concerning the matter have often been embellished, he nonetheless affirmed that certain persons were predestined to destruction and eternal damnation.[17] This is not to assume that sinners (according to Calvin) are innocent. They rightly deserve their condemnation because of their sin. However, the non-salvation of reprobates is also due to God's foreordination; in other words, he wills their reprobation.[18] God does not merely leave sinners in their unfortunate state; he hardens them unto that state, as he did with Pharaoh. As in passive reprobation, no consideration is given to foreseen faith or works, because the involvement of human faith or works as a cause would imply that salvation would then be merited and grace nullified. As vessels prepared for destruction, sinners (under double predestination) are actively predestined for eternal torment.

Numerous alternatives to the problem of implicated evil in reprobation have been proposed. Some, such as the Lutheran Formula of Concord in 1577, accept the positive side of predestination (whereby God predestines the elect to salvation) while rejecting its negative side, which amounts to reprobation by immutable decree.[19] William of Ockham equated predestination with foreknowledge of free decisions (a matter to be discussed below under the category of conditional election).

Additionally, after John Calvin, a debate arose on the ordering of the divine decrees. Did God first decree to save the elect and then decree the fall (*supralapsarianism*) as Theodore Beza contended, or did God first permit the fall and then elect some to salvation and others to condemnation (*infralapsarianism*, associated with François Turrettini)?[20] More recently, Karl Barth boldly applied reprobation only to Christ, 'the Elect of God who is also the bearer of the divine rejection'.[21] This interpretation, for Barth, leaves open the possibility of universal hope for humanity and preserves human responsibility.[22] Still other theories, such as Middle Knowledge and open theism, can be described as further attempts to resolve

---

Kirkpatrick, 'Unconditional Election and the Condemnation of Sinners: An Analysis of Eric Hankins's View of Reprobation', *Journal of Baptist Theology and Ministry* 16, no. 2 (Fall 2019): 47–48.
17 Calvin, *Institutes*, 3.21.1–7.
18 Cornelis P. Venema, 'Predestination and Election', in *Reformation Theology: A Systematic Summary*, ed. Matthew Barrett (Wheaton: Crossway, 2017), 257.
19 See Wolfhart Pannenberg, *Systematic Theology*, vol. 3, trans. Geoffrey W. Bromiley (Grand Rapids: Eerdmans, 1998), 446, where he notes that Concord did not dichotomize election and reprobation as one and the same act but affirmed that one's rejection was sourced in foreseen guilt.
20 Carl R. Trueman, *Grace Alone: Salvation as a Gift of God*, ed. Matthew Barret (Grand Rapids: Zondervan, 2017), 148–49, highlights how supralapsarianism and its corresponding reprobation inject harsh arbitrariness to God's nature that is unreflective of God's goodness found in Scripture.
21 Karl Barth, *Church Dogmatics*, ed. G. W. Bromiley and T. F. Torrance (Peabody, MA: Hendrickson, 2010), II/2/§35, 409.
22 Shao Kai Tseng, 'Condemnation and Universal Salvation: Karl Barth's "Reverent Agnosticism" Revisited', *Scottish Journal of Theology* 71, no. 3 (2018): 326, 331–32, 338. See also Thomas F. Torrance, 'The Atonement, the Singularity of Christ and the Finality of the Cross: The Atonement and the Moral Order', in *Universalism and the Doctrine of Hell: Papers Presented at the Fourth Edinburgh Conference in Christian Dogmatics*, ed. Nigel M. de S. Cameron (Carlisle: Paternoster, 1991), 157. Torrance affirms (with Barth) that God does not reject sinners to hell, but says that sinners may choose to refuse the election of grace and subsequent rejection in Christ.

the problem that reprobation seems to implicate God with evil and challenges God's goodness.[23]

The problem of implicated evil

The most common argument against reprobation is that it lacks justice towards humanity, dooming the condemned to hell not because of their sins but because God rejected them or actively destined them to that end. Kenneth Keathley, arguing against this notion, states, 'In this paradigm God does not reject the reprobate because he is a sinner; it is the other way around. The reprobate becomes a sinner because God rejected him.'[24] Or consider this definition of double predestination by R. C. Sproul: 'God's decreeing from all eternity that certain unfortunate people are destined for damnation'.[25] Here, the cause of the damnation is clearly God.

Such statements understandably lead people to question the goodness of God's justice. The Reformed tradition would generally agree that justice is a character trait found in God himself as he seeks to uphold his righteous law and condemn sinners *for their sin*.[26] God must punish those who rebel against his law, and to do so is justifiable retribution. Yet in reprobation, punishment for one's own sin is exactly what is *not* happening. Sinners are not condemned (at least not exclusively) for their rebellion but for being rejected. They are tormented not just because of their sin but because of divine decree. By definition, both active and passive reprobation locate the source of eternal condemnation in the acts of God, not the sinner.

Let us return to the Greek word *adokimos*, which refers to a failure to measure up to a test. The term, as employed by the biblical authors, does not refer to foreordained eternal demise. There must, then, be a clear distinction between reprobation and retribution (as theologically defined). Reprobation (as defined above) is condemnation based upon the will of God and established in eternity past. Retribution, on the other hand, is condemnation based upon the defiant actions of the person carried out in real time. Scripturally speaking, sinners are said to receive punishment for their sins and are condemned (*katakrinō*) accordingly. The biblical authors base such condemnation and punishment solely upon sinners breaking the

---

[23] Middle Knowledge, also known as Molinism in light of its founder Luis de Molina, is the belief that God, infinite in knowledge, could choose from any possible worlds from which to create, knowing what free creatures would do under those designs. Thus, he remains sovereign but creatures remain free. Open theism (associated in recent years with Clark Pinnock and Gregory Boyd), on the other hand, claims that God limits his knowledge of the future so that humans remain free. Both of these theories seek to solve the problem of reprobation by immutable decree, believing that it implicates God with evil.

[24] Kenneth Keathley, *Salvation and Sovereignty: A Molinist Approach* (Nashville, TN: B&H Academic, 2010), 143. The second statement made here is questionable, though the former has merit. In reprobation, God would be the cause for one's demise, though one need not say that a person becomes a sinner because of God's rejection.

[25] R. C. Sproul, *What Is Reformed Theology?* (Grand Rapids: Baker, 1997), 157.

[26] See Augustus Hopkins Strong, *Systematic Theology* (Philadelphia: Judson Press, 1954), 292–93, who affirms that God's justice, established in his divine nature, mandates that he punish sinners for their sin. If sinners are punished for their sin, there is no problem; however, if they are punished not for their sins but simply for God's good pleasure, it is argued that such implicates God's moral character.

law of God (both by nature and by choice). Thus, condemnation is caused by humanity, not God. Reprobationists equate reprobation with retribution, yet the two should remain distinct (particularly since the biblical term does not align with their definitions of reprobation).

Here, one who holds to passive reprobation might object that God's goodness need not be challenged, for God can condemn sinners for their sin and (at his own discretion) save certain ones from peril while leaving the rest of them in it. However, as noted above, in passive reprobation the sinner is not specifically condemned for his or her sin. Louis Berkhof clarifies this point by stating, 'Preterition [i.e., passive reprobation] is a sovereign act of God, an act of His mere good pleasure, in which the demerits of man do not come into consideration. ... The reason for preterition is not known by man. It cannot be sin, for all men are sinners. We can only say that God passed some by for good and wise reasons sufficient unto Himself.'[27]

Berkhof's explanation is revealing, for he acknowledges that in this view sinners are *not* passively rejected because of their sin, but for God's own reasons. Whether one holds to active or passive reprobation, one ultimately has to conclude that sinners are condemned on the basis of God's will, not human disobedience. This would seem to be an act of injustice that would implicate God's character.

Some, such as James White, interject Romans 9:20-22 at this point. White contends that some 'vessels' (persons) are prepared for eternal destruction simply because God is free and sovereign. He has absolute right over his creation to do as he pleases.[28] Whether Romans 9 refers to individuals for all time or a segmented people group at a specific point in history will not be argued here.[29] But as White's example illustrates, many advocates of reprobation agree with their critics that God is (at least in part) the cause of a sinner's eternal peril.

Although not entirely distinct from the accusation against God's justice, a second common accusation is that reprobation makes God evil in both source and deed. Arminius forcefully criticized the idea that God 'wills the greatest evil to his creatures; and that from all eternity he has preordained that evil for them'. For Arminius, such reprobation would implicate God with evil, because there was nothing external to the will and affection of God to cause him to take this action.[30] That is, God would be choosing, of his own initiative, that people should do acts of evil as a means to bring about their condemnation.

Roger Olson also observes that such hard predeterminism makes God the author of sin, evil and suffering (even the Holocaust, for example) while calling into question God's goodness and loving nature.[31] Persons would have no choice but to sin, for God would have made them that way. The sin committed in the Garden of

---

27 Louis Berkhof, *Systematic Theology* (Grand Rapids: Eerdmans, 1976), 116-17.
28 James R. White, *The Potter's Freedom* (n.p.: Calvary Press, 2009), 212-15.
29 For this argument, see Eric Hankins, 'Romans 9 and the Calvinist Doctrine of Reprobation', *Journal of Baptist Theology and Ministry* 15, no. 1 (Spring 2018): 62-74.
30 Arminius, 'On Predestination', 1:166 for both quotations. See also J. Matthew Pinson, 'Jacobus Arminius: Reformed and Always Reforming', in *Grace for All: The Arminian Dynamics of Salvation*, ed. Clark H. Pinnock and John D. Wagner (Eugene, OR: Resource Publications, 2015), 158-59.
31 Roger Olson, *Against Calvinism* (Grand Rapids: Zondervan, 2011), 84. See also Olson, *The Mosaic of Christian Belief* (Downers Grove, IL: InterVarsity Press, 2002), 191.

Eden would be an inevitable necessity, along with its spread to all humanity. Yet Scripture is abundantly clear that sin finds its source in human beings, and that this very sin, not God's immutable decrees, serves as the basis for their condemnation (Lk 13:27–28; Jn 3:18; Rom 2:6–8; 6:23; Rev 21:8).

In the terminology of most Western courts, the injustice found in God according to the deterministic account described above would be the solicitation of evil. A person who commits a crime may be held responsible for his or her actions, but the law also considers whether that person was forced or induced to commit that crime. It is one thing to be found guilty of sins one has wilfully committed, but it is quite different if the sinner is forced or programmed to act in a way that leads to condemnation. Such a situation would not establish God's justice, as the strongly Reformed may wish to claim; rather, God would be implicated with injustice for compelling other beings to engage in evil acts.

Conditional soteriology is not the answer

Thus far, to make the case that the doctrine of reprobation unacceptably implicates God with evil, I have appealed to many Wesleyan/Arminian and non-Reformed theologians. I will now consider how this tradition views the basis for the condemnation of sinners. For most within the non-Reformed community, the more attractive alternative is to make salvation conditional, with faith as the condition to be met.

Roger Olson, a prominent Arminian, is adamant on this point: 'But Arminians want to make clear that persons reprobate themselves; God does not really damn anyone, especially unconditionally.'[32] Through a libertarian understanding of free will, enabled by prevenient grace, one is presented with the opportunity to believe and accept Christ or reject him as Lord and Saviour (thereby placing the blame of condemnation solely upon the unrepentant sinner).[33] Most, if not all, aspects of salvation are conditioned upon the person exercising faith (enabled by prevenient grace) prior to the desired outcome being realized. Thus some, such as Eric Hankins and Norman Geisler, see election as conditioned upon faith (so as to avoid reprobation).[34] Others affirm that conversion must occur prior to regeneration, so that any blame for a lack of faith rests upon the sinner, not upon God for not making them regenerate.[35] Redemption is also viewed conditionally so as to avoid

---

32 Roger Olson, *Arminian Theology: Myths and Realities* (Downers Grove: IVP Academic, 2006), 180.
33 Olson, *Arminian Theology*, 36, 53, 71, 180; Keathley, *Salvation and Sovereignty*, 86–91, 104–8.
34 Hankins, 'Romans 9', 92; Norman Geisler, *Chosen but Free: A Balanced View of Divine Election* (Minneapolis: Bethany House, 2001), 67–73.
35 Ronnie W. Rogers, 'Commentary on Article 5: The Regeneration of the Sinner', in *Anyone Can Be Saved: A Defense of 'Traditional' Southern Baptist Soteriology*, ed. David L. Allen, Eric Hankins and Adam Harwood (Eugene, OR: Wipf and Stock, 2016), 78; Steve W. Lemke, 'A Biblical and Theological Critique of Irresistible Grace', in *Whosoever Will: A Biblical-Theological Critique of Five-Point Calvinism*, ed. David L. Allen and Steve W. Lemke (Nashville, TN: B&H Academic, 2010), 117–27.

implicating God with the evil associated with reprobation.[36]

However, such a position presents its own set of complications. Consider the notion of cause and effect and its relation to salvation and works. There is an efficient cause (the source or agent that brings about a particular change) and an instrumental cause, i.e. 'a secondary cause that produces the effect which owes its efficacy to the efficient cause'.[37] Although various traditions argue for synergism (or two forces working together) in the efficient cause—which, in this case, would conflict with the idea that salvation is all of grace—more commonly the synergism is placed within the instrumental cause. God is the efficient justifier, regenerator, elector and redeemer, it is claimed, but he does not do his work until a person cooperates by exerting faith.[38]

At this point, the Reformed have good reason to be suspicious of such conditional soteriology. The instrumental cause of salvation, in this reasoning, is the human act of faith. However, for the Reformed, the source of salvation cannot be located in the sinner, for then such salvation would not be entirely by grace.[39] Salvation is indeed through faith, but not because of it; all is owed to grace. Faith is a receptive instrument by which God works some of the aspects of salvation, and it is a necessary component, but it does not *cause* salvation (for then the salvation would be by works).[40] Moreover, if faith is a cause of one's salvation, it would seem to follow that a lapse of faith can undo one's salvation, causing concern for those who hold the doctrine of eternal security.

In this article, I seek to uphold two convictions: that salvation is entirely of God's grace independent of human causes, and that the doctrine of reprobation as presented above is not acceptable. On one hand, one is entirely saved by God, who serves as both efficient and instrumental cause; although faith may be an instrumental means applicable to some aspects of salvation, it cannot be considered a cause, for that would mean that salvation comes by human activity. On the other hand, the doctrine of reprobation implicates God with evil and is not a viable explanation. How can we reconcile these two positions?

Reconciling unconditional salvation and just condemnation

Is it consistent to argue that one's condemnation is attributable to a person while affirming that salvation is not? In this section, I will argue for this view. My purpose

---

36   Robert E. Picirilli, 'The Intent and Extent of Christ's Atonement', in *Grace for All: The Arminian Dynamics of Salvation*, ed. Clark H. Pinnock and John D. Wagner (Eugene, OR: Resource Publications, 2015), 52–55; David L. Allen, 'The Atonement', in Allen and Lemke, *Whosoever Will*, 65, 76, 94–96; F. Leroy Forlines, *Classical Arminianism: A Theology of Salvation* (Nashville, TN: Randall House Publications, 2011), 193.

37   Daniel Kirkpatrick, *Monergism or Synergism? Is Salvation Cooperative or the Work of God Alone?* (Eugene, OR: Pickwick, 2018), 17.

38   Such faith is not sheer self-effort, it is claimed; no claims of Pelagianism are warranted, given the notion of prevenient grace. By divine enablement, a person is able to choose Christ for salvation, leading to either personal salvation or deserved condemnation.

39   Trueman, *Grace Alone*, 41–44; see also Kirkpatrick, 'Unconditional Election and the Condemnation of Sinners', 52.

40   Kirkpatrick, *Monergism or Synergism?* 39–44; Kirkpatrick, 'Unconditional Election and the Condemnation of Sinners', 52.

is to provide a defensible alternative that does not implicate God with the evil associated with reprobation as described above.

As already noted, God should be viewed as the efficient cause of all aspects of salvation. Most non-Pelagians hold this view, although synergism in the efficient cause is maintained by some non-Reformed. Although he is the source of all saving activity as efficient cause, God still works instrumentally to accomplish the various aspects of salvation. The instrumental means varies depending upon the soteriological aspect. Those of Reformed leaning affirm that faith is not instrumental on the sinner's part with regard to such aspects as election, regeneration and redemption while readily admitting that some aspects (such as justification) involve the human activity of faith. For the passive aspects of salvation, God would be the efficient cause while the instrumental cause would be his divine will, decree or action. For active aspects such as justification, God works by means of that faith to justify the sinner, though such faith did not effectually cause the justification.

Those of a less Reformed leaning affirm that salvation (in most or all of its aspects) is conditioned upon the instrumental cause of faith. For them, our election, redemption, regeneration and the like depend on the exercise of human faith, apart from which there would be no realization of those aspects. Although it is readily affirmed that such an action is non-meritorious, it is nonetheless a condition that the person must meet for salvation to be realized.

Although I cannot discuss this issue in detail here, I have argued elsewhere that human causation in either efficiency or instrumentality amounts to salvation by works and nullifies the fulness of grace.[41] Although sinners are justified by faith, they are not justified because of it. God's choice of sinners has nothing to do with foreseen faith or goodness but solely His good pleasure. As enslaved persons, we cannot cause our own redemption, just as spiritually dead persons cannot cause their own regeneration apart from divine initiative. Holding strictly to a monergistic perspective in the efficient and instrumental causes, one may most consistently affirm salvation as being all of grace.

But how can a monergist affirming unconditional salvation avoid the problems of reprobation as mentioned above?[42] Reprobation, whether active or passive, assumes that God is the efficient and instrumental cause of damnation. I claim that in this case, God would be implicated with evil for condemning a person on unjustifiable grounds. However, if the cause of condemnation remains in the sinner, and if the sinner is sentenced and judged for his or her own sin, then God would not be implicated with evil and would remain a just judge.

As attested in Scripture, God condemns sinners on the basis of their sin and disbelief (not his good pleasure).[43] The sinner, thus, is the efficient cause of sin carried out instrumentally through evil and perverse actions and attitudes, resulting in unbelief and a rejection of the Messiah. God would be the efficient cause of judgement but, like an earthly judge, would incur no guilt in issuing a condemnatory

---

41 See Kirkpatrick, *Monergism or Synergism?*; Daniel Kirkpatrick, 'An Exegetical and Theological Argument for the Priority of Regeneration in Conversion', *Mid-America Journal of Theology* 31 (2020): 89–101.
42 For my full treatment of this issue, see Kirkpatrick, 'Unconditional Election'.
43 Kirkpatrick, 'Unconditional Election', 52–53; see 1 Pet 1:17; Col 3:25; Rev 20:11–15.

verdict over infractions of the law. The sinner remains solely responsible for his or her sin and deserving of the consequence.[44]

Yet this alone does not solve the problem. Does not holding to unconditional soteriology necessitate an acceptance of reprobation?[45] One author, an adamant proponent of conditional soteriology, claims that if unconditional election were true, God would be requiring individuals to express faith but then denying them the very ability to have faith (and condemning them for that lack of faith), which ultimately amounts to reprobation anyway.[46]

Note, however, that this charge does not fit the definition of reprobation. Even in this critique, sinners are still condemned for their own sin, even if they are unable to reach for the cure. God can condemn persons for failing to believe in his Son for salvation, yet this does not make God the efficient or instrumental cause of that unbelief. The sinner, in this case, broke the divine law and failed to accept the cure. God remains just and unimplicated with evil. Furthermore, one need not say God withholds the ability for a person to believe. Sin did that, and such sin was committed by the sinner, resulting in a just condemnation.

Another author uses an analogy, comparing the non-elect to children caught in a fire. A fireman goes in graciously and saves some, but it was within the fireman's capacity to save more children. Although it was good that the fireman saved some, he did not save all he could have reached (which would cause one to question the fireman's goodness). Similarly, the argument runs, God arbitrarily saved some when he could (should?) have saved more.[47]

However, this is a gross misrepresentation of the issue. Sinners are not helpless orphans tragically caught in a burning building. They are rebels against the one true King.[48] They are not people who inwardly want redemption from Christ yet lack the capacity to embrace it. They are haters of God and his Son Jesus, hostile by nature and choice.[49] Though they certainly do not desire eternity in hell, they do not want

---

44 I do not hold the view that all human behaviour is foreordained by God; rather, I view it as volitional, rendering persons responsible for their decisions. All human behaviours and decisions, however, are affected by sin and render the person free only to do what is non-meritorious before God. Thus, humans (as a consequence of their own actions) are in a depraved state that calls only for God's justice, not redemption. By God's grace, however, he provides redemption to the elect. For development of this view, see D. A. Carson, *Divine Sovereignty and Human Responsibility: Biblical Perspectives in Tension* (Eugene, OR: Wipf and Stock, 1994), 195–98. See also Greg Welty, 'Election and Calling: A Biblical Theological Study', in *Calvinism*, ed. E. Ray Clendenen and Brad J. Waggoner (Nashville, TN: B&H Academic, 2008), 225–27.

45 Hankins, 'Romans 9', 62 claims it is a 'necessary corollary'. Michael F. Bird, *Evangelical Theology*, 2nd ed. (Grand Rapids: Zondervan Academic, 2020), 565 finds reprobation to be the corollary of unconditional election by divine predestination.

46 Braxton Hunter, 'Commentary on Article 8: The Free Will of Man', in Allen, Hankins and Harwood, *Anyone Can Be Saved*, 121–22, 125–26.

47 Steve W. Lemke, 'A Biblical and Theological Critique of Irresistible Grace', in *Whosoever Will*, 148–49.

48 See Kirkpatrick, 'Unconditional Election', 54–55.

49 An objection to the effect of having one's cake and eating it too (wanting to appeal to divine sovereignty for salvation but human responsibility for condemnation) may be raised. However, this dilemma would apply only if one were to affirm divine sovereignty to the neglect of human

to acknowledge Christ as King. God remains fully justified for condemning them in their sin; thus, there is no reprobation or implication of evil.

Another objector may argue as follows: if all people are depraved and incapable of coming to Christ for salvation on their own, and if God regenerates the hearts of some, leading to the salvation of only the foreordained elect, is not God implicated with evil, and does not all this amount to reprobation anyway? The answer is no on both counts.

For active reprobation to occur, God would have to condemn someone solely for his good pleasure and glory—creating people as sinners destined to wrath simply to manifest God's justice. As has already been argued, this is not a matter of justice but a perversion of it, for in this rendition sinners would be condemned not for breaking God's law but because of God's decree. The view I have presented does not fit that description, for it says that sinners are condemned on the basis of their wilful sin and lack of belief.

My view also does not fit the definition of passive reprobation, in which the efficient cause of the sinner's condemnation is God, expressed instrumentally via divine rejection. Although I acknowledge that God chooses some and passes over others for salvation, I reject the notion that sinners are condemned *because* they were passed over. Rather, sinners were permitted to do exactly what they want to do (which is to sin and rebel against God) while rejecting God's sole means of salvation (which is Jesus Christ). Non-Calvinists affirm this as well.

Moving now to what is likely the heart of the issue, if one were to hold to unconditional salvation as proposed here, would God be implicated with evil if he transforms the hearts of the elect only and not all persons? Does this deny his universal love for all people or his alleged desire that none should perish but that all should come to repentance (2 Pet 3:9)?

First, changing things to a conditional soteriology does not solve this issue. If salvation were based upon what a sinner has done, salvation is of works, grace is nullified, and it would be only a matter of time before a sinner's choices undo his salvation. Rather, salvation is secure because it rests in what God has done rather than what a sinner has done.

---

responsibility (which is not the view affirmed here). As stated above, human beings are the efficient and instrumental causes of sin. While God serves as judge and condemner of sin, he is not culpable for human sin, for such sin and demise (I contend) were not preordained. The nature of divine justice mandates that God must punish sin; it does not mandate that he must save sinners. This would be non-necessitated grace. Thus, as mentioned above, God does not preordain human sin, though he does preordain salvation (foreknowing the fall and electing according to his intentions). There is a qualitative difference, as argued in the fireman analogy, between orphans in a burning building and rebels who volitionally switched allegiances to become God's enemies. Humans are responsible for their sin (deserving just condemnation), thereby dispelling notions of reprobation. Just condemnation (the view argued here) is different from foreordaining condemnation (the reprobationist view). Choosing to let people to incur the consequences of their wilful behaviour is not the same thing as foreordaining their behaviour or demise (and thus there is no reprobation). This view is argued by E. Earle Ellis, *The Sovereignty of God in Salvation* (New York: T&T Clark, 2009), 1–17; Carson, *Divine Sovereignty and Human Responsibility*, 195–98; Bruce Demarest, *The Cross and Salvation* (Wheaton, IL: Crossway, 2006), 135–38.

Second, one must look to what God's perfect moral nature is required to do. God's just character mandates that he judge sinners, not that he must save them. The law of God (broken by sinners) mandated condemnation for all, not salvation for all. If God were obligated to save, that would lead to universalism. God can still love people who rebelled against him despite having to give them just condemnation.

Finally, God is not implicated with evil because he did not reprobate. Although I grant that God transforms the hearts of the elect and not all persons, this is not reprobation, because God would still be condemning people for their wilful sins, not for being passed over. They are not innocent bystanders inwardly wanting salvation; rather, they are hostile in heart and deed to the things of God. God is under no obligation to save anyone, and though he chooses to save some people without any reference to any merit found within the sinner, he is absolved of all guilt when he condemns sinners for their sin.

Conclusion

Most Christians are unlikely to attempt such a rigorous philosophical reconciliation between our role in salvation or damnation and God's justice as I have sought to construct here. However, all of us need to be prepared to defend God's justice. I have summarized the historical and recent concerns of those who find a belief in reprobation to be implicating God with evil. I have also shown how modern theologians attempt to bypass the problem of reprobation through a belief in conditional salvation. To me, neither reprobation or conditional salvation is acceptable. However, I have attempted to establish that we can view God as totally, unconditionally responsible for the salvation of sinners without making God unjustly responsible for the fate of the reprobate who reject God.

Luther's Peculiar Doctrine of the *Imago Dei*

Geoffrey Butler

Martin Luther believed that through Adam's fall, humanity lost the image of God, which is restored only through justification by faith. That doctrine would imply that non-Christians do not have the image of God in them. This paper analyses Luther's argument and proposes a mediating position: all humans retain the divine image, but only justification can restore the divine likeness.

Justification by faith is the theological distinctive most closely associated with Martin Luther. Indeed, he considered it so integral that he once asserted, 'This article, how we are saved, is the chief of the whole Christian doctrine, to which all divine disputations must be directed. … God has declared no article so plainly and openly as this.'[1] In the opening of *The Disputation Concerning Man*, his most significant text addressing theological anthropology, Luther argues that the very definition of what it means to be human is tied to justification, citing Paul's claim in Romans 3:28 that 'man is justified by faith.'[2] He claims the 'essence' of humanity is found in being justified by faith in Christ, and, according to Marc Cortez, he depicted justification in such a way that it 'sheds light on the entire spectrum of human existence'. Luther's understanding of justification by faith envisions this doctrine as holding implications far beyond soteriology, stretching to eschatology, creation and more.[3]

Luther's unique approach raises numerous questions. Did Paul mean what Luther claims in his interpretation of Romans 3:28? What does Scripture or Christian tradition prior to Luther say about the notion that humanity's identity and the related issue of the *imago Dei* are inextricably linked to justification?

Although we should approach all theological questions with humility, the image of God especially demands it because of the lack of scriptural detail indicating precisely what the image entails. As Millard Erickson explains, 'The Bible teaches us that God created humans in his own image and likeness. Though there are some

---

Geoffrey Butler is a PhD student at Wycliffe College, University of Toronto and a teaching assistant at Tyndale University.

---

1 Martin Luther, *The Table-Talk of Martin Luther*, ed. William Hazlitt (Grand Rapids: Christian Classics Ethereal Library, 2004), 200.
2 Martin Luther, 'The Disputation Concerning Man', in *Luther's Works*, ed. Jaroslav Pelikan (St. Louis, MO: Concordia, 1958), 34:139.
3 Marc Cortez, *Christological Anthropology in Historical Perspective* (Grand Rapids: Zondervan, 2016), eBook, chap. 3.

general indications of its nature, we are not able to determine from Scripture what the image of God involves specifically.'[4]

In this paper, I argue that though Luther's great zeal to defend the doctrine of justification by faith and bring it into conversation with theological categories beyond soteriology is commendable, as is his desire to construct an anthropology that is thoroughly God-centred, we should not tie justification to the image of God as Luther did. His view, if taken to its logical conclusion, could have rather serious unintended consequences regarding how Christians view unbelievers. However, I propose that if we modify Luther's position and place it in dialogue with the traditional substantive view—the position articulated by most of the church fathers and medieval theologians who preceded him—his doctrine of the *imago Dei* nevertheless holds the potential to make a fruitful contribution to the ongoing discussion.

Luther's position

Given Luther's rampant zeal for the doctrine of justification by faith, it is fitting that he was enthusiastic about integrating it with his anthropology. Before we further explore that relationship, however, we must establish exactly how he understood the *imago Dei* and the relationship of justification to it.

As noted above, Luther's anthropology is, paradoxically, nothing if not God-centred. Richard Lischer described Luther's attitude towards the study of man in this way: 'Every misunderstanding begins with an attempt to analyze the human being and human freedom in isolation from the person's relationship to God in the crucified Christ.'[5] In other words, for Luther, proper anthropology must be primarily theological; it is impossible to separate an understanding of the human person from an understanding of God. It seems fair to say that humanity is not even the core focus of Luther's anthropology!

It may be helpful to frame Luther's theology in light of Augustinian influence, since he served as an Augustinian monk prior to assuming an indispensable role in the Protestant Reformation.[6] It is difficult to miss the influence Augustine's thought exerted upon the reformer; like the patristic giant before him,[7] Luther also asserted that the likeness of God in humanity was lost in the Fall and could be fully restored only through personal salvation.[8] Yet Luther went further than Augustine in

---

[4] Millard J. Erickson, *Introducing Christian Doctrine*, ed. L. Arnold Hustad (Grand Rapids: Baker Academic, 2015), 10.
[5] Richard Lischer, 'Luther's Anthropology in Dialogue', *Currents in Theology and Mission* 11, no. 5 (October 1984), 282.
[6] For an in-depth biography of Luther's life, including an overview of his time as an Augustinian monk, see Heiko Augustinus Oberman, *Luther: Man Between God and the Devil* (New York: Image Books, 1992), 124–29.
[7] Matthew Puffer, 'Human Dignity after Augustine's "Imago Dei": On the Sources and Uses of Two Ethical Terms', *Journal of the Society of Christian Ethics* 37, no. 1 (2017): 73.
[8] Stanley J. Grenz, *The Social God and the Relational Self: A Trinitarian Theology of the Imago Dei* (Louisville, KY: Westminster John Knox, 2001), 163–64. Grenz notes that Luther's desire to articulate the doctrine of the image of God in a different light than his medieval predecessors 'was occasioned by his concern for the restoration of what he deemed to be the New Testament gospel'.

explicitly denying that the unregenerate retain the divine image in any sense; it is not just that the likeness has been taken away, but the very image.[9] In a 2017 article discussing Augustine's theological anthropology, Matthew Puffer makes a striking statement that helps to illustrate where Luther breaks with his patristic predecessor:

> Three times in *De Trinitate* 14, Augustine repeats that the image of God is this capacity in human nature for participation in God as opposed to the active participation itself. The capacity is intrinsic to and inherent in human nature such that it is not lost even when this capacity is not activated, not operationalized by God's love as the Holy Spirit. Thus, the old, unregenerate, *sub lege* human (of Colossians 3 and Ephesians 4) is just as much the image of God as is the new, regenerate, *sub gratia* human.[10]

Herein lies a crucial distinctive of Luther's position. Augustine viewed the image of God as something intrinsic to humanity, but Luther flatly rejected this approach.[11] Likewise, although Augustine, like many of the church fathers, makes a crucial distinction between the image and likeness of God, Luther does not. Thus, his position is much less hospitable to the nuance that often characterizes the church fathers on this topic.[12] Moreover, Augustine asserted that though the image may not be 'activated'[13] in the unbeliever, it nevertheless remains present, an assertion Luther denied. In fact, in his 1535 *Lectures on Genesis*, Luther launched a full-blown assault on medieval and patristic thought concerning the *imago Dei*—including that of Augustine—precisely on the grounds that they look for something internal within human beings that constitutes the image.[14] Luther declared this idea 'foolish'.[15]

Following Luther's line of reasoning, if the image is not something intrinsic, it must consist of something external to the human person; on this basis, it becomes much easier to claim that the image can be totally lost. So completely did the Fall

---

His project was to articulate a view distinct from the commonly held 'structural understanding'— i.e. that certain capabilities such as reason or will in the human person constitute the essence of the divine image.

9   Grenz, *The Social God*, 164.
10 Puffer, 'Human Dignity', 74.
11 Martin Luther, 'Lectures on Genesis, Chapters 1-5', in *Luther's Works*, 1:60-61.
12 Grenz, *The Social God*, 164.
13 See Augustine, *The Trinity* 14.14:4, in *The Works of Saint Augustine*, ed. John E. Rotelle, trans. Maria Boulding, 2nd ed. (Hyde Park, NY: New City Press, 2012), I/5, where he asserts, 'But that image of the Creator, that has been implanted immortally in its own immortality, must be found in the soul of man, that is, in the reasonable or intellectual soul … even when it is most wretched—so even though reason or intelligence is now dormant in it, or now appears to be small and now great, yet the human soul is never anything but reasonable and intellectual.' Augustine, in short, makes the case that since human beings in their natural state can exercise the capacity to reason, even the 'most wretched' still retain the divine image.
14 Grenz, *Social God*, 164.
15 'To me', Luther declared, 'their statement would appear to be far more correct if they said that the image of God in man disappeared after sin in the same way the original world and Paradise disappeared. … When we must discuss Paradise now, after the Flood, let us speak of it as a historical Paradise which once was and no longer exists. We are compelled to discuss man's state of innocence in a similar way' ('Lectures on Genesis', 1:90). Thus, for him, the image of God is lost just as the Garden of Eden has been lost to us. The divine image cannot be recovered apart from divine redemption, in the same way that creation itself cannot be restored apart from divine action.

wipe out God's image, Luther asserted, that humans can no longer truly comprehend what the image in all its fulness entailed—nor will we be able to do so during our earthly lives.[16] Consistent with his assertion that the image of God is directly linked to justification by faith, he proposed that when Genesis spoke of Adam bearing the *imago Dei*, it indicated that in the Garden he 'lived a life that was wholly godly'.[17]

Although Luther's conviction that humanity lost the image of God in the Fall might imply that he held a rather low view of humanity, this description of Adam prior to the original sin shows clearly that this pessimism pertains only to his postlapsarian state. Therefore, modern interpreters of Luther must be careful to distinguish his view of Adam before the Fall from his state afterwards; as Karl Barth observed, the Reformed tradition has 'never spoken about God and man as if God were everything and man were nothing',[18] and Luther is no exception. Rather, he viewed the Fall as radically corrupting a human nature that was originally noble and upright.

This contrast has led some observers to comment that, for Luther, humans in their true form are 'so fashioned in God's image that they are fully responsible for carrying out God's plan and will for human living',[19] suggesting that Luther's view of the human person is, in fact, not hopelessly pessimistic. However, he has a sweeping view of the effect of the Fall and of human sin. Allen Jorgenson indicates that for Luther, the image of God essentially consists of two qualities: living without fear of death and 'being content with God's favor'.[20] Regarding the latter quality, Jorgenson explains:

> To know the favor of God is to know that God sees you as a child born from her own womb and so bearing something of God's own character. The favor of God is, for Luther, both God's gracious gaze upon her children and what that gaze renders. ... The human is lovely not because of our intrinsic loveliness, but because God's look renders the human lovely.[21]

---

16 Luther, 'Lectures on Genesis', 1:90.
17 Luther, 'Lectures on Genesis', 1:63. He asserts that Adam 'was without the fear of death or of any other danger, and was content with God's favor ... if they should transgress His command, God announces the punishment: "On whatever day you eat from this tree, you will die by death", as though He said: "Adam and Eve, now you are living without fear; death you have not experienced, nor have you seen it. This is My image, by which you are living, just as God lives. But if you sin, you will lose this image, and you will die."' Thus, he understands God's warning to Adam not to eat from the tree as a warning that doing so will result not only in physical death, but in the loss of the *imago Dei* in addition.
18 Karl Barth, *The Knowledge of God and the Service of God According to the Teaching of the Reformation, Recalling the Scottish Confession of 1560*, Gifford Lectures, 1937-1938 (New York: AMS Press, 1979), 35.
19 Robert Kolb, 'God and His Human Creatures in Luther's Sermons on Genesis: The Reformer's Early Use of His Distinction of Two Kinds of Righteousness', *Concordia Journal* 33, no. 2 (2007): 166.
20 Allen Jorgenson, 'Beyond Luther's *Imago Dei*: Imagining a Modest Humanity', *Canadian Theological Review* 3 (2014): 70-71.
21 Jorgenson, 'Beyond Luther's *Imago Dei*', 71.

Those who are justified can truly be said to bear the image of God because they are objects of his divine love and therefore may live fully content, without fear of death or danger.

To summarize Luther's position, justification is tied to the *imago Dei* in that it restores what was lost in the Fall. The faith which effects justification once again 'creates God's image in the believer'[22] that was previously destroyed, allowing the faithful to rest in the knowledge that God looks upon them with favour. This allows Christians to live in light of his love until they see Christ face to face. Luther's understanding of the image of God is grounded in creation but has a thoroughly eschatological element inherent in it as well.

A potential overstatement?

As the Protestant tradition is so deeply indebted to Luther on the matter of justification by faith, it may seem perilous to question some of the implications he drew from his commitment to this doctrine. However, in the case of his understanding of the divine image, such criticism is necessary. First, Luther's claim that the statement 'Man is justified by faith' in Romans 3:28 refers to the image of God seems to be opportunistic exegesis. There is little in the text itself or in the Christian tradition of interpretation prior to Luther to support the notion that Paul has the *imago Dei* in view here.[23] Some observers have proposed that part of Luther's zeal to link humanness with justification flowed from the crushing burden to perform according to medieval church standards in order to enjoy the grace of God—a burden that many Germans of his time wrestled with.[24] Thus, one could understand why Luther may have overstated the case for his theological anthropology. Nevertheless, there is no indication in the context of Romans 3 that the apostle is theologizing about the *imago Dei*; rather, Paul is countering the Jewish notion that one could be justified before God via obedience to the Law.[25] Thus, to use this text to prove one's theology of the image of God is simply inappropriate.

Second, Luther often seems quite dismissive, even cavalier, in his interaction with patristic and medieval perspectives on this topic. Granted, had he not been

---

22 Antti Raunio, 'Martin Luther and Cajetan: Divinity', *International Journal of Philosophy and Theology* 78, no. 1–2 (2017): 56.

23 One helpful resource on this question is Jeffrey P. Greenman and Timothy Larsen, eds., *Reading Romans through the Centuries: From the Early Church to Karl Barth* (Grand Rapids: Brazos Press, 2005). Although the book does not contain a chapter specifically on Luther, the chorus of voices quoted from throughout church history—including some, such as Calvin and Wesley, who shared Luther's zeal for the doctrine of justification—none view Paul's teaching on the subject as intrinsically linked to the divine image as Luther did.

24 Robert Kolb, 'Luther's View of Being Human: The Relationship of God and His Human Creatures as the Core of Wittenberg Anthropology', *Word & World* 37, no. 4 (2017): 332.

25 For a brief overview of Paul's purpose in writing this passage, see Roger Mohrlang, Philip W. Comfort and Gerald L. Borchert, *Romans* (Carol Stream, IL: Tyndale House, 2007); Timothy George and Scott M. Manetsch, *Romans 1–8*, ed. Gwenfair Walters Adams (Downers Grove, IL: InterVarsity Press, 2019). Like most commentaries, neither one considers 3:28 as holding implications for the *imago Dei*. Both, however, comment on Luther's doctrine of justification, with the latter noting at Romans 3:28 that 'Luther's translation of the Bible into German was criticized for adding the word "alone" to the end of this statement, but his rendering accurately conveys the meaning of the text in its context.'

willing to plant his flag in the ground and affirm rather unpopular positions, the Reformation as we know it likely would not have occurred. Indeed, one of the leading reasons why Luther came to be recognized as an indispensable figure in early Protestantism was his willingness to challenge the ecclesiastical establishment. Nevertheless, he seems too quickly dismissive of historic voices on the matter of the *imago Dei*, including those to whom he was greatly indebted on other topics. Even Augustine, for whom he routinely expressed great admiration, is dismissed as 'foolish' for his openness to the idea that the image of God may still be present in some intrinsic human quality.[26] This may be one area where Luther's legendary stubbornness, documented by numerous Luther scholars and church historians, may have gotten the better of him.[27]

Finally, the most obvious element of Luther's position that must be questioned concerns the nature of unbelievers. Is it true that non-Christians do not bear the image of God? Besides the fact that the Genesis 3 text, which details the Fall, never states or even hints that Adam and Eve lost the *imago Dei* as a result of their transgression, other texts of Scripture long after the Fall clearly affirm the universal bestowal of the image on all humanity. Notably, after Noah steps off the ark following the catastrophic flood, the Lord declares to him that 'Whoever sheds human blood, by humans shall their blood be shed; for in the image of God has God made mankind' (Gen. 9:6, NIV). According to Old Testament scholar Victor Hamilton, there is 'no evidence here that sin has effaced the divine image. It is still resident in the post-flood, post-paradise man.'[28] This is no small admission considering the context; so great was the depravity of mankind during this time as to evoke drastic divine judgement. Yet there is no exception or limit to the sweeping statement that humans are made 'in the image of God'—presumably even including the wicked, about whom Luther adamantly insists that they do not bear the *imago Dei*.

How then shall we think? An alternative proposal

Perhaps Luther's view that unbelievers did not possess the image of God can be blamed in part for his mistreatment of certain people groups in his own lifetime, including the virulent anti-Semitism that has come to plague his legacy.[29] So deep-seated was this theme in his writings that the Nazi party used them to justify their attempted genocide of the Jewish people. As recently as 2014, Luther's work *On the Jews and Their Lies* was reprinted by an American fringe group with a history of

---

26 Luther, 'Lectures on Genesis', 1:90–91. He responded to Augustine's exposition in *De Trinitate* by urging believers to read 'the opinions of the Fathers'—however valuable—'with discretion'. Though commending much of Augustine's work, Luther nevertheless charged him with leaning too much on Aristotle in his doctrine of the *imago Dei* with the result that he retained Aristotle's understanding of the image as directly related to 'the powers of the soul'.
27 Oberman, *Luther: Man Between*, 298.
28 Victor P. Hamilton, *The Book of Genesis: Chapters 1–17*, New International Commentary on the Old Testament (Grand Rapids: Eerdmans, 1990, eBook), chap. 9.
29 Michael L. Brown and Mazal Holocaust Collection, *Our Hands Are Stained with Blood: The Tragic Story of the 'Church' and the Jewish People*, 2nd ed. (Shippensburg, PA: Destiny Image, 2018), 31–32.

promoting anti-Semitic conspiracy theories.[30] Poor theology can have dire consequences. Of course, as the shortcomings of many other Christians throughout history make clear, sound theology does not ensure proper treatment of others. Yet Luther's straightforward denial that unbelievers—those who are not justified by faith—also bear the image dispenses with a massive incentive to treat all persons with dignity and respect. Thus, even beyond scant biblical support, this view of the *imago Dei* appears deficient from a moral standpoint.

But if we reject Luther's position, where should one turn for an alternative? I would suggest turning to the distinction between image and likeness proposed by several church fathers, including Augustine as cited above. It is truly surprising that Luther would reject the distinction between image and likeness, given some of his other theological distinctives.[31] Luther would readily affirm, for example, that one's standing before God is a different matter from one's similarity to Christ in terms of character or behaviour; his doctrine of justification by faith alone assumes that even when believers fall into temptation, the righteousness of Christ remains theirs.[32] Thus, it would seem that we can link justification by faith with restoration of the *imago Dei* without coming to the unpleasant (and unbiblical) conclusion that a large portion of humanity no longer bears the divine image. Luther's doctrine of justification still has immense potential to enrich this alternative. His desire to link justification and theological anthropology could help explain how, though all humanity retains the *image* of God, through justification by faith the *likeness* of God is restored in the believer. Ironically, one of the best places to begin developing this alternative is the very composition with which Luther took issue: Augustine's classic *On the Trinity*.

There is substantial motivation for looking to the patristic period, and Augustine in particular, to enrich the discussion surrounding justification and theological anthropology. His position neither downplayed the disastrous effects of the Fall on humanity nor claimed that unbelievers do not bear the *imago Dei* in any sense. Augustine accomplished this balance through his distinction between image, in the sense of rationality and capability of having a relationship with God—something possessed by all humanity—and likeness or resemblance, which can be restored only through an active relationship with God and is thus possessed only by the believer.[33] In this way, Augustine follows many other patristic authors, such as Irenaeus and Tertullian, who posited a distinction between the image and likeness of God—the former, retained after the Fall, encompassing such faculties as reason and freedom of the will, and the latter shattered by the Fall, capable of restoration only by

---

30 See Brown, *Our Hands Are Stained*, 33-34.
31 Luther's objection ('Lectures on Genesis', 1:61) that locating the image in some internal quality, such as reason or free will, means even Satan could be said to bear the image is a worthy objection that I address briefly below. However, this alone does not seem a sufficient reason to resist the distinction between image and likeness.
32 Luther, *Table Talk*, 193–94.
33 See Claudia Welz, 'Imago Dei', *Studia Theologica—Nordic Journal of Theology* 65, no. 1 (2011): 79, https://doi.org/10.1080/0039338X.2011.578372. Welz claims that Augustine 'clung to the idea that the image of God in the human mind is indestructible and needs only a renewal after the Fall and remains capable of this *reformatio* in that the human mind can remember, understand and love the one who has created it'.

'supernatural endowment' that believers alone enjoy when in communion with God.[34] On this account, it is possible to hold simultaneously that all people are divine image bearers, thus possessing inherent dignity, and that something significant—human likeness to God—was lost in the Fall and can be recovered only through a restored relationship with him.

It is precisely here that Luther's doctrine of justification could make an indispensable contribution. Luther's theological anthropology, we have noted, is unrelentingly God-centred. It is greatly concerned with how humanity relates to God and insists that doing so properly may be accomplished only through faith. For Luther, the chief cause of the Fall was a lack of trust, or doubt that God's word was in fact true. This, consequently, resulted in disobedience, the breakdown of the relationship between God and humanity, and the loss of the divine image in the latter.[35] We could partially accommodate Luther's understanding by saying that justification involves the restoration of the likeness of God, with the image of God being retained even by the unbeliever.

According to Luther scholar Robert Kolb, the reformer would give this explanation to his students when lecturing on Genesis 3:

> Disobedience of God's commands arises from doubting his promise and defying his person; it mars and destroys their relationships with other human beings and the rest of creation. The original sin that compelled the expulsion of Adam and Eve from the garden only confirmed their own act of expelling themselves from the relationship God created for himself and them. Since that relationship consisted of trust, doubt is the original sin.[36]

If the sin which effaced the likeness of God in humanity and deprived humans of the 'supernatural power' to which the church fathers referred was in fact doubt or lack of trust, it would make sense that the thing which would restore that likeness should be the opposite—namely faith, which, in Luther's thought, is the effective cause of justification. Therefore, if one makes the distinction that Luther rejects—between image and likeness—but applies his line of reasoning to restoring the *likeness* of God in the fallen human being rather than the image, the potential exists to transform a position with deeply troubling implications into a fruitful theological concept. The assurance of divine love and one's standing before God could be reimagined as constituting part of the divine likeness rather than the image, thus retaining the essence of Luther's position while avoiding some of its troubling implications. Luther's emphasis on the role of faith in conforming the believer to the image of Christ should not be overlooked or rejected outright on account of some other flaws.[37] Rather, by recovering the image/likeness distinction that he mistakenly

---

34 See Michael F. Bird, *Evangelical Theology: A Biblical and Systematic Introduction* (Grand Rapids: Zondervan, 2013), eBook, chap. 7. Bird notes, 'According to Irenaeus and Tertullian, humanity lost the "likeness of God" at the fall, but retained the "image of God". It was only through the renewing power of the Holy Spirit that the likeness was restored.' The position of Irenaeus and Tertullian that the likeness of God is restored by the Holy Spirit could be strengthened by understanding justification as the way in which God initiates and sustains this process.
35 Kolb, *Luther's View*, 330.
36 Kolb, *Luther's View*, 334.
37 Raunio, 'Martin Luther', 56.

rejects, we can uphold Luther's zeal to link justification with the divine image without coming to the unpleasant conclusion that not all humans retain the image of God.

In Luther's shoes: potential objections

What objections might Luther's defenders raise against this proposal? Those who object to a universalist soteriology, for instance, might protest that under my reconstruction of Luther's theology, many bearers of God's image will ultimately be lost. Consequently, they may prefer Luther's position that believers alone enjoy the divine image. Alternatively, those who share the great reformer's zeal to promote justification by faith may fear that this proposal does not adequately emphasize the doctrine on which, for Luther, the church stands or falls—an understandable objection given the recent 'Protestant Exodus',[38] as Phillip Cary terms it, of many evangelicals to Eastern Orthodoxy and Roman Catholicism. Finally, Luther's aversion to grounding the image of God in anything intrinsic to the human person is indeed understandable; if capabilities for relationship and knowledge of God are vital to the *imago Dei*, as many suggest, then even Satan, Luther protests, 'was created according to the image of God, since he surely has these natural endowments'.[39]

I will respond briefly to these objections. First, since Luther himself did not hold to the later Calvinist position that salvation cannot be forfeited—often termed 'perseverance of the saints'—it seems that he and those who share his position are in a serious dilemma as well.[40] What do we say about an individual who is once justified by faith but subsequently abandons the faith? Would that person retain the image of God even while in a state of condemnation? Or do those who leave the faith lose the divine image once again? Can the *imago Dei* be lost and regained multiple times? Not only would such a conception trivialize the divine image altogether, but it would provide little comfort for Christians who struggle with doubt. In addition, since Genesis refers to the image of God only in the context of humanity's vocation on earth, perhaps the doctrine's implications for the afterlife are beyond what Scripture seeks to address in any case.

Second, regarding the centrality of justification by faith, we should recognize that going beyond what Scripture teaches is never an appropriate way to defend any doctrine, no matter how vital. Luther, after all, was quick to criticize the Catholic Church of his era for doing just that on such matters as transubstantiation, withholding communion from the laity, and misinterpreting biblical passages to fit its particular understanding of the Eucharist.[41] Overstating the significance of

---

38 Phillip Cary, *The Meaning of Protestant Theology: Luther, Augustine, and the Gospel That Gives Us Christ* (Grand Rapids: Baker Academic, 2019), 2. Cary has observed this trend amongst those with an increasing awareness of and love for the great tradition of Christian thought, particularly his own students.
39 Luther, 'Lectures on Genesis', 1:60.
40 Cary, *The Meaning of Protestant Theology*, 249–50. Cary suggests that whenever one debates whether one can lose salvation, 'You know you're listening to Protestants downstream from Calvin', since for Luther the only irreversible entry point to the Christian life was baptism.
41 William R. Russell, editor's preface to Martin Luther, 'The Babylonian Captivity of the Church: Part I', in *Martin Luther's Basic Theological Writings* (Minneapolis, MN: Fortress, 2012), 196.

justification on scant exegetical grounds, ironically, might even weaken Protestants' ability to promote it at all. Moreover, the fact that justification by faith is not directly tied to whether one bears the image of God does not make it irrelevant to soteriology; my alternative proposal retains it as essential to the restoration of the divine likeness.

Regarding Luther's objection to grounding the *imago Dei* in any natural endowment, it seems that the reformer overstated his argument when he claimed that in this case even Satan could be said to bear the image. Nowhere in the Genesis narrative are angels, animals or anything else in all creation said to enjoy the special relationship with God that Adam and Eve enjoyed. They are given the role of co-regent over the rest of creation, a point Michael Bird masterfully articulates in what he calls the 'royal view' of the image of God, wherein humans are fashioned as God's representatives to the rest of creation in the way that ancient Near Eastern monarchs placed physical depictions of themselves all over their kingdom to express their authority.[42] To reject Luther's position on justification and the image of God, therefore, does not require the extreme conclusion that Satan too is endowed with the image; indeed, this appears to be more a product of Luther's propensity to hyperbole than of careful exegesis or logical necessity.

Reasoned, critical dialogue is the best response by those who, while differing from Luther on particulars as I have done here, still see him as an indispensable source for theological retrieval. Luther himself could have been expected to support attempts to reform even our deepest theological commitments by examining them in the light of the Word of God. Our discussions of how the *imago Dei* remains present in humans should be conducted in this spirit.

Conclusion

Luther's articulation of the doctrine of justification by faith should be enthusiastically celebrated and the man himself should be honoured for recovering such a pivotal doctrine. His imperfect conception of the *imago Dei* should not cause us to overlook the many ways in which the church has benefitted from Luther's influence. Though we should not adopt his model uncritically, its redeeming qualities should inform the Christian's theological anthropology. However, we must avoid the untenable and dangerous assertion that only Christians bear the divine image.

With Luther as with all other great figures of Christian history, the contemporary church must learn from both the insights and mistakes of those who came before us, while allowing their views to help us identify our own shortcomings as well. I hope this paper has provided a good illustration of how to let Christian thinkers of previous eras inform our thinking while remaining attentive to areas where they may have departed from sound theology.

---

42 Bird, *Evangelical Theology*, chap. 7.

Book Reviews

Vern S. Poythress, *The Mystery of the Trinity:*
A Trinitarian Approach to the Attributes of God

David Hunsicker, *The Making of Stanley Hauerwas:*
Bridging Barth and Postliberalism

Shao Kai Tseng, *Immanuel Kant*

Tom Holland, *Dominion: The Making of the Western Mind*

The Mystery of the Trinity:
A Trinitarian Approach to the Attributes of God
Vern S. Poythress

Phillipsburg, NJ: P&R Publishing, 2020
Pb., 667 pp., index

Reviewed by Dallas B. Pitts, Assistant Professor of Religion, Baptist Health Sciences University, Memphis, Tennessee, USA

In recent years, many books on the Trinity have been published, such as ones on the doctrine's historical development or how it is understood from various theological persuasions. Those books are much needed, and so is Poythress' work, which interprets the Trinity in relation to the attributes of God.

Each attribute is considered systematically, with special attention to how the attributes are at the core of God's trinitarian nature. At over 600 pages, the result is not short, but as systematic works should be, it is thorough in scope.

The book begins with knowing God and classical Christian theism, and it ends by answering challenges to Christian theism. Along the way, Poythress includes substantial sections on the Trinity and language as well as on philosophical problems.

Parts 1–3 of the book contain scriptural affirmations and a discussion of the attribute being explored or the argument being advanced. Along with responses to common questions, Poythress relates each attribute of God to the resurrection and to our practical experience, making his presentation valuable both theologically and pastorally. This particular feature is worth the price of the book in my opinion, as few books on the Trinity devote as much space to the resurrection of Jesus or the application of God's attributes to humans as God's image-bearers.

Key terms are listed in each chapter and defined in a glossary; Poythress also provides study questions, a bibliography for further reading and a concluding prayer. The book's structure is quite similar to that of Wayne Grudem's *Systematic Theology*.

The first three of the book's eight parts focus directly on God's attributes. In part 4, on language and the Trinity, Poythress begins by showing how the resources of language and thought find their foundations in God; as God speaks, so humans, made in God's image, speak by imitation. Poythress discusses Scripture's use of anthropomorphisms to help humankind understand God's attributes. In this way, language functions to compare God to created things as a way for us to understand his attributes and complex personality.

Part 5 considers technical terms related to the Godhead, such as essence and substance, and the mistakes that occur when we misunderstand the concepts these terms represent. Poythress ends this section with an admonition to pursue clarity in terminology.

Parts 6 and 7 return to the topic of Christian theism. Beginning with a chapter on 'Aristotle's Unmoved Mover', Poythress explores the differences between the Unmoved Mover and the Christian God, most notably that Aristotle's system leaves no place for a trinitarian God. He draws contrasts between Christian and non-Christian theism, showing how Aristotle's Mover concept lacks the real ability to explain God when compared with God as revealed in the Bible. After that, Poythress endeavours to follow the progression of Aristotelian thought in Christian theology from Aquinas to the Reformers and Puritans, particularly Stephen Charnock. These chapters help to uncover the problems that result when Aristotelian philosophy is used to explain Christian theism, in contrast to seeking to establish the trinitarian doctrine of God and his attributes based on Scripture alone.

Part 7 presents ways to deal with challenges to the position outlined in part 6. Through nine chapters, Poythress explains how knowing God on his own terms, apart from non-Christian philosophical categories, keeps us from dissolving God's unity or inadequately distinguishing his attributes in the language we used for God. Poythress discusses the difficulties entailed in describing God's nature and the Trinity's action in the world, arguing that the Christian view of transcendence and immanence, accompanied by the trinitarian action of the three persons of God in the world, is the only real way to know God, especially in Christ. Ultimately for Poythress, many of the challenges posed by non-Christian views of immanence and transcendence are countered through the revelation of God in Christ and justified by the resurrection.

In the eighth and final part, Poythress resumes the structure used in the first three parts of the book. Here he highlights the particular attributes of love, mercy, will and knowledge in connection to the resurrection. Poythress urges the reader to submit all questions about God's nature to the authority of the Bible, but also to grow and gain insight from the perspectives of the past. He reminds us that all true perspectives about God through the ages are in harmony, because 'God harmonizes with himself.'

The Making of Stanley Hauerwas: Bridging Barth and Postliberalism
David Hunsicker

Downers Grove, IL: IVP Academic, 2019
Pb., 248 pp., fwd., bibliog., index

Reviewed by Francis Jr. S. Samdao, Teaching Fellow, Philippine Baptist Theological Seminary, Baguio City, Philippines

Stanley Hauerwas is one of the prolific thinkers of our time; *Time* magazine called him the 'best theologian in America' in 2001. Not surprisingly, he has attracted legions of followers as well as critics. In this book, David Hunsicker reckons with those critics who call Hauerwas a Protestant liberal. To do so, he examines the claim that Hauerwas is a Barthian and scrutinizes the critics' arguments, concluding that Hauerwas is a Barthian postliberal.

Hunsicker is well qualified for the task, as Hauerwas himself affirms in a foreword to the book. He serves as an adjunct professor at Azusa Pacific University.

Hunsicker classifies the criticisms into two main arguments: the Schleiermacher thesis and the Ritschl thesis. The former concerns Nicholas Healy's depiction of Hauerwas' theology as *ecclesiocentric*—i.e. as reducing theology to ecclesiology, much as Schleiermacher reduced theology to feelings. The latter refers to the claim by John Webster and Nigel Biggar that Hauerwas reduces Scripture to a guide for the church instead of a form of witness to God's activity.

In chapters 1 and 2, Hunsicker discusses the influence of Barth and postliberals on Hauerwas so as to explicate why he denies the Constantinianism of liberal Protestantism. Hauerwas also denounces the syncretism between Christianity and Americanism. Therefore, he rejects the notion that the fundamental task of ethics is about America, emphasizing that it should be about developing a community of character.

Chapters 3 and 4 argue that Hauerwas is a faithful follower of Barth, as demonstrated by his rejection of universal reason as the main fulcrum of ethics. Instead of discussing abortion in the public square, for instance, he starts with Christian identity as a premise, thus making the church the locus of the discussion. Hauerwas opines that the fundamental basis for rejecting abortion is not the principle of respect for life, but God as the source of life. Also, he goes beyond Barth by emphasizing ecclesiology, albeit holding to the vitality of Christology since 'the church is always the church that recognizes Christ's lordship' (169).

In Hunsicker's view, Hauerwas' postliberal theology fills a gap in Barth's theology. Whereas the Schleiermacher thesis critiques this move by Hauerwas, Hunsicker defends this use of a postliberal lens to interpret Barth. In fact, he says that Hauerwas, by following Barth, has managed to keep ethics and dogmatics together due to the resources he borrows from his predecessor's works. However, Hauerwas finds Barth's ethics very abstract, so he reconfigures it from being merely a witness to Christ into making theological discussion as part of the church's life and practice. In this way, the Christology of Barth and the ecclesiology of postliberalism create in Hauerwas the spirit of a Barthian postliberal.

After dealing with the Schleiermacher thesis, Hunsicker turns to the Ritschl thesis, examining the relationship between the church and Scripture in the thinking of both Hauerwas and Barth. Hunsicker explains that although Hauerwas' focus is on the church and Barth's was on God, this does not make the former an ally of Schleiermacher and the other Protestant liberals, because his ecclesiocentrism is rooted in a Barthian perspective. Overall, Hunsicker presents the possibility of reading Hauerwas' ecclesiology as a partner to Barth's Christocentric theology.

Hunsicker brings a wealth of scholarship and astounding knowledge, as attested in his hermeneutical analysis and his use of primary sources, to this well-written book. His training under Hauerwas and his conversations with other thinkers who hold similar perspectives make his arguments penetrating and insightful. The publisher's use of footnotes rather than endnotes makes the additional comments contained in the notes more accessible to the readers. Readers who are not acquainted with Barth and Hauerwas will benefit significantly from these extended critical comments.

On the other hand, the book's great erudition is also a limitation. Hunsicker seems to assume that his audience has read some of Hauerwas' work and is knowledgeable in historical theology. As a result, readers unfamiliar with the theological context of Barth and Hauerwas would struggle to join the ongoing conversation. Readers with less background could helpfully engage with this book in conjunction with Nicholas Healy's *Hauerwas: A (Very) Critical Introduction* so that they can more effectively weigh the arguments and counter-arguments.

Immanuel Kant
Shao Kai Tseng

Phillipsburg, New Jersey: P&R Publishing, 2020
Pb., 209 pp., glossary, bibliog., indices

Reviewed by Elmer John Thiessen, retired instructor of philosophy, Medicine Hat College, Canada

This book is part of a Great Thinkers series edited by Nathan Shannon from Seoul, South Korea. The series introduces thinkers who have had a profound influence on our present age and assesses them from a Reformed perspective. The 16 volumes listed, including five that are forthcoming, cover philosophers from Plato to Plantinga, theologians from Karl Barth to Karl Rahner, political and economic theorists from Marx to Adam Smith, and skeptics Nietzsche and Richard Dawkins.

Author Shao Kai Tseng (familiarly known as Alex Tseng) is research professor in the philosophy department of Zhejiang University, Hangzhou, China. He self-identifies as a neo-Calvinist theologian and historian of Christian thought, with graduate degrees from Regent College, Princeton Theological Seminary and Oxford.

In the first of this book's three chapters, Tseng explains 'why Kant matters today'. He describes Kant's *Critique of Pure Reason* as 'the most important work of philosophy to have been written in modern times'. Unfortunately, Kant is 'notoriously difficult' to read, let alone understand. (I know—I rather foolishly chose to write my MA thesis on Kant's notion of God.) Tseng argues that Kant has been misinterpreted by many Christians, including traditional Calvinists such as Abraham Kuyper, Herman Bavinck and Cornelius Van Til.

Chapter 2, the longest chapter, attempts to summarize Kant's thought, beginning with the intellectual-historical context of Kant's works. Tseng then helpfully analyses the *Critique of Pure Reason*, showing how Kant tried to safeguard science, morality and religion from the threat of empiricist skepticism that grew out of Descartes' rationalistic philosophy. Tseng's careful discussion of how Kant reconstructed epistemology helped me to appreciate the positive aim behind Kant's famous statement that he was critiquing reason 'in order to make room for faith'.

The final section of this chapter covers Kant's treatment of practical reason as applied to theology, morality and hope. Reading Tseng forced me to re-evaluate my earlier assessment of Kant as an agnostic. Although we cannot have theoretical knowledge of God, Kant argues that we can and indeed must postulate the ideas of God, freedom and immortality on practical grounds and for practical purposes. Kant even acknowledges the Bible as divine revelation, though he downplays its historical dimension. But in the end, Kant wants a rational religion focussed on morality, one in which the sacrifice of human effort in doing good is itself seen as a form of atonement.

Tseng labels Kant as a Christian, not an agnostic. I'm not convinced. Of course, it all depends on how one defines 'Christian'. But Christians surely want to say more than that 'God ought to exist'. Though we cannot know God fully, Christians maintain that we can have knowledge of God in Christ, as Tseng himself highlights in his conclusion.

The third chapter assesses Kant's thought from a Reformed perspective. Though Kant tried to make room for faith, he did so by separating faith from reason and so undermined the possibility of theology being a science. Tseng gives us a grand tour of subsequent philosophers and theologians who have tried to reclaim theology as a science, while noting that Kant and his successors set the stage for 'the diverse and complex tradition of modern liberal theology'. Tseng, along with other Reformed thinkers, follows Anselm in proposing that 'faith and understanding are not two different forms, but two stages of knowledge.' In the faith-seeking-understanding tradition, faith is the beginning of knowledge. 'Theology as a science, then, begins with faith in the self-revealed God.'

Tseng provides a helpful introduction to Kant and some of the controversies in Kantian scholarship. But just like Kant himself, this book is not an easy read. Tseng spends much time defining key concepts used by Kant, which is hard to avoid, but I would have liked to see more big-picture analysis. Tseng does an impressive job of showing how Kant's thinking intersects with that of other philosophers and theologians, though sometimes I felt the connections were carried too far. Nonetheless, I found the book helpful in providing an incisive critique of Kant from a Reformed perspective. I also appreciated the charitable tone exhibited in Tseng's interaction with the secular academy, which is described as 'instituted by God's common-grace design'.

Dominion: The Making of the Western Mind
Tom Holland

London: Little Brown, 2019
(American edition: *Dominion: How the Christian Revolution Remade the World*)
Pb., 697 pp., bibliog., index

Reviewed by Jim Harries, missionary in east Africa and adjunct faculty member at William Carey International University, Pasadena, USA

The impact of Holland's easy-to-read bestseller, replete with historical incidents expressed as stories that draw on his skill as a novelist, is demonstrated by the numerous podcasts, reviews and discussions of the book available on the web. Holland, an accomplished historian shocked by the cruelty of antiquity, wondered what has made the world the compassionate place that it is today. He discovered the cause in Christianity.

That Jesus could be both a victim of crucifixion, one of the many torturous techniques that maintained the power of empires in antiquity, and also the Son of God was from the beginning 'scandalous, obscene, [and] grotesque'. This understanding, which Holland articulates by drawing on the apostle Paul, became the 'single dominant set of beliefs' in Europe, and it has resulted in Western life and even language up to the present time being 'shot through with Christian connotations' (all three quotations from the preface).

Christianity mushroomed in the Roman Empire despite persecution and became official under Constantine, who oversaw the setting of boundaries on its doctrines, thus honing its role as a massive, original, 'fissile source of power' (Kindle location 2388) with global aspirations. The life of total devotion to Christ in monasteries, which came to be known as *religio*, later became the desirable life for all believers. The papacy acquired greater power than kings had. Scribes serving the popes brought them more influence than armies could have done. They enabled appropriation of Roman law into the church, recognizing that 'God's order was rational' (4129) and, from Aquinas, that all 'wisdom was Christian' (4528). Later, due to Luther's preference for grace rather than law to fulfil the 'yearning … for purity' (5649) in reformed churches, church-honed law eventually became a part of what came to be known as secularism.

Although indeed popes and, subsequently, diverse Christian powers have committed violence, Holland points out that, as a result of their knowledge that their own falsely accused Lord allowed himself to be cruelly slaughtered to save mankind, their violence was consistently accompanied by a 'pall of anxiety' (5198). Christians came to value 'toleration' (6189). Using Jesuit activity in China as an example, Holland shows that a distinctive Christian outlook on the world underlay the development of modern science and technology.

The very dynamic of renewal and reformation that Christianity inaugurated, and which contributed to Protestant rebellion against Catholics, later re-emerged, spearheaded by Voltaire, as a secular rebellion against the gospel itself. Benjamin Franklin realized that the best way to promote Christian values was to not call them Christianity! Human rights and endless other expressions of contemporary democratic liberal and secular life were fashioned with their Christian origins carefully concealed. Non-Christian ways of life—Hinduism is one example given by Holland—became Christianized without being brought to faith in Christ, through a secular 'neutrality' considered by Holland to be a 'conceit' (7156).

Holland portrays Darwinism as a threat to what had become a very powerful Christian impulse in favour of the weak, the suffering and the marginalized. Nowadays, ironically, Christianity is blamed by some for bringing patriarchalism to a world in which those untouched by the gospel are romantically seen as innocent and noble. That 'nothing in this narrative was true' (7497) has not prevented it from being popular. The Beatles' famous song, 'All You Need Is Love', did not come to them through scouring the Scriptures, Holland tells us. They merely took its acceptability for granted; the original gospel source had become hidden. Yet in other parts of the world (Holland cites Africa as an example) where Christianity was expected to decline after colonial and missionary withdrawal, the church instead proliferated, proving the scholars wrong. Christianity is a powerful, vitalizing movement even outside the West. Meanwhile, its impact on the West itself has been so profound as to render it hidden.

The fact that Holland's research and writing is not that of a Christian apologist but of a secular historian ready to tell the truth adds to the value of this book. Reading it is a profound experience. It sheds light on avenues of possibility in historical causation that contemporary secular historians have been intentionally avoiding. Christianity, which is fundamentally about believing in Jesus, is indeed a world-changing movement that continues to give direction to many contemporary developments throughout the globe. Holland's depiction of this process is a phenomenal read that pierces one's soul with renewed hope.

www.ingramcontent.com/pod-product-compliance
Lightning Source LLC
Chambersburg PA
CBHW070516090426
42735CB00012B/2807